bare

The MISPLACED ART *of* GRIEVING *and* DANCING

Sandy Oshiro Rosen

BIG TREE PUBLISHING
LANGLEY, BC

Published by Big Tree Publishing, Langley, BC Canada
ISBN 978-0-9937030-1-0

www.sandyrosen.com
www.bigtreepublishing.com

Edited by Lesley Cameron
Design by Patrice Nelson
Photo by Kevin Clark

contents

preface

i must begin this book with an expression of gratitude, not only for the willingness of the many individuals who had the courage to tell their stories, but also for their willingness to share them publicly with the reader. Names and identifying details have of course been changed to protect these individuals, all of whom have graciously given me permission to share some of the most vulnerable moments of their lives.

I have included some of my own stories as well, though initially I did not anticipate that I would have had so much to tell. Life unfolds in the most unexpected ways, and although the book sprang almost entirely from the story of my friend's unfathomable loss and grief, it was the sudden experience of my own losses that I believe has brought authenticity to my observations and commentaries.

This is very much a personal take on grief and grieving. By no means do I claim or assume that my perceptions are entirely objective, but I have taken these personal narratives and set them alongside professional perspectives in order to explore the process of grief as fully as possible. I recognize that those with firsthand experience of grief and loss often have a more precise understanding of the effects, the challenges, the struggles, and the stalemates that emerge as grief lingers than the clinical experts do. It is why these stories matter. Those who weather extreme sorrow have much to offer to the rest of us.

The idea to write this book came from the realization that not only do we have difficulty in processing our own grief, but we have also become a culture that does not know how to grieve. We North Americans do not grieve well with one another and we do not often permit grieving as an acceptable, often time-consuming aspect of real life. It is for that reason that I have added a sociological, sometimes anthropological bent to my discourse. Since we have lost an appropriate concept of grieving in this culture, in short, we have *misplaced* our understanding of grieving and need to find it again, I sense a need for re-education. An undercurrent of dance permeates the book, and I hope that will provide a fresh and buoyant approach to this vexing feature of life's passage.

Further, as one who daily confronts the physical manifestations of grief in the bodies of dancers, I have also added a physiological dimension to the book. Current experts such as Gabor Maté have dared to propose that many chronic illnesses can frequently be traced back to an experience of trauma, often in childhood, in the lives of the ailing—that is, pain literally gets trapped in the body. I have taken this discussion a little further by reasoning that if our grief has a bodily manifestation, then our response to grief should logically have a physical expression in order to facilitate soul-relief. It is not an original idea—mourning and dancing have been paired for millennia—but what might be new is that North Americans have, for the most part, partitioned dance as a trivial diversion rather than the powerful force that I would suggest it is, particularly as connected to grief.

I have come to understand this because of the dancers who have generously shared their lives and their creativity with me. Their sharing was of an intensity that I'm sure none of them would have originally aspired to, nor necessarily desired to. I cannot thank them enough for their generosity.

Words cannot begin to express my unending gratitude for my family—both my extended family and my nuclear one. To have parents, siblings, in-laws, and children who equally embrace creativity, faith, love, and authenticity is an indescribable gift. To my daughters, dancers, and warriors against injustice: you have endured much and tolerated much, but I pray these difficulties will only deepen your compassion for others, increase your artistic breadth, and strengthen your determination to use all that you are to transform the world around you. To my husband, my partner in sorrow: it has been a tumultuous 30 years, but you have proven true and tenacious. Thanks for being by my side through all of it with wisdom, tenderness, innovation, and encouragement.

And to Vanessa, my friend through this life-renovating process of grieving and dancing: You have been my educator, my companion, and my inspiration, all simply by being one who loves and grieves deeply. As you have said yourself, sorrow and loss are not things we experience and then presume to be *done with*—they are constants in life, and it is the calm periods between loss episodes that remind us to be grateful for all we have. Being a dancer, you expertly demonstrate beauty through your moving body—it is one of my primary joys—but the greatest beauty you shared with me was in the tiny quiet face that we saw but never knew. Her beauty spilled out into our lives in the form of your resonant vulnerability, your honest sorrow, and your immense grace. It has been a beautiful pain. Thank you for allowing me into it.

And finally, as a point of detail, the references in the book include links to talks and videos—I would encourage you to avail yourself of these. The references have been divided into printed resources and online links that were viable and accurate at the time of printing. Thank you for picking this book up. With all that is out there, I recognize it is no small thing that you are willing to invest your invaluable time with me. I hope that this proves an enriching experience.

Sandy Oshiro Rosen
June 27, 2014

1

good grief

*t*he pain had begun with slowly intensifying waves, rising and rolling in gentle succession, but then they grew, mounting and crashing over her, unrelenting—body, soul, and spirit were now under siege, her very being pushed beyond its capacity to prevail. The pain was unfathomable. She heard the giddy voices of her parents just outside her room as if in a dream. Their joy contrasting sharply, surreally with the terrible wall of agony that had erected itself on her foundation of peace. She would need to focus, endure.

The prospect of a new baby always elicits a mixture of emotions—excitement and fear, thrill and suffering—but for Vanessa, the mixture was not what she had envisioned. Now dread had unaccountably been added. With her husband gripping her hand, she braved each aching wave that coursed through her body, tight-lipped and silent as labored minutes ticked by.

And then it was done. The voice of the nurse in the hallway, inviting her family, "You can come in and see the baby now." Excited babble rising as they entered the room. But not her room. The bulge of her baby-belly was still and full with child. Her heart was swelling with anguish. She restrained herself from crying out, "Here I am!" But in this moment, they would not even know she was there. In this moment, their joy was for her sister's baby, newly born in the hospital room across the hall.

Today would not be her day for the euphoria of birth, of new life—today would be a day of grief so deep it would form a crevice in her soul. What kind of cruel, divine joke had been played out? What twist of fate had aligned the timing and location of her loss with that of her sister's blessing?

This was the true, unfathomable experience of my dear friend Vanessa. She was a mere week away from the birth of her first child when she sensed that all was not well. The previously active tiny baby girl inside her had ceased her squirming, and lay still in her mama's womb all that day, prompting an emergency trip to the hospital. Although Vanessa and her sister were due to have their first babies three weeks apart, and at different hospitals, at the very moment Vanessa was being told that her baby had died, her sister was giving birth to a son in the same hospital, at the same time—and directly across the hall from her examination room. Her parents would not know about this dreadful coincidence until later.

Vanessa's grief over her loss lingered and lingered, weeks, months, years ... Every family celebration for her nephew's birthday would be a searing reminder of the anniversary of her loss. As I walked alongside my friend through this trauma, and wept with her through its catastrophic and unexplainable aftermath, there was an overwhelming fog of unanswered *why*'s that stripped us all of our bearings, spiritually, emotionally, relationally. Numbness reigned.

Our introduction to grief and grieving

As a dance instructor in the studio I own, Vanessa would sometimes arrive at class showing evidence of a night rendered sleepless by emotional torment, her grief assaulting her. I had made an agreement with her at the beginning of the year. When she had lamented, just weeks after the loss of her baby, Mattea, "I really don't think I'm up for teaching this year—I'm still in so much pain," I had responded, "It's all right. Just keep coming, and if you can't teach on any given day, we will just sit and cry with you."

And we did. On several occasions, mid-class, she would crumple to the floor in a bawling heap, cradled in a welcoming lap, as one young woman after another would pray for her, coddle her, massage her aching limbs, weep for her, weep with her. Whatever they could offer in comfort, they would. Of the key elements of comfort offered, the most unexpectedly effective was dance. When her pain had no voice, when there were no words to express all that she was feeling, one of the dancers would begin to dance spontaneously over her. Her grief seemed borne by the flow of the arms, by the gestures of the hands, by the articulation of the torso, by the stoop of the shoulders, by the bending of the legs. Unleashed, her tears would stream. Those were the most beautiful and moving times any of us had ever experienced. Over the next months, which turned inevitably into years, dance would become our companion, our guide—a mystifying and persistent interpreter of grief.

Loss and dance

This remarkable experience began to give us new insight: that our grief is meant to be a shared thing. In the case of Vanessa, it was evident that she could not grieve on her own; she truly needed our help. It was the first time that any of us had understood that there is an important communal dimension to our grieving. We were not very skilled at navigating this journey—we had not experienced much loss—so her grieving was to become our first classroom. There was also a nagging sense that we should take note of what we were seeing, hearing, and sharing. This experience was showing us something; it seemed as if the timing and occurrence of her situation (the loss of her baby paired with the birth of her sister's) had almost been deliberate, part of a grander plan to prevent us from dealing lightly with grief. We seemed consequently prepped to learn things about grief we had never understood before.

For me, it was to be the beginning of a five-year degree, a master's as it were, in grieving. At some point during Vanessa's ordeal, I even recall breathing something as audacious as, "I thank God that I really haven't experienced much loss in my lifetime." This observation was poised to come back and bite me. My experience of grief was about to become firsthand through multiple deaths and a near-death. In my grief, I would experience the pain of abandonment, the aloneness of grieving in solitude, and the gift of a caring community.

I was also about to understand how, throughout my life on a whole other series of levels, there had been times when I had been preparing, hoping, dreaming, *pregnant with vision* as it were, for something, only to have the whole thing miscarry just as it was about to be birthed. Across life's hallway, someone close to me was being blessed with the very thing that had now been lost to me: relationships I hoped would endure, but fell apart; projects I poured my life into and that crashed before they were accomplished; trusted overseers who deceived or took advantage of me. I had seen the aftermath of losses of all sorts—from divorce to natural disasters to genocides—that left lives reeling.

I have compiled a series of stories from a selection of grievers and combined them with personal reflections on loss in an effort to resurrect approaches and methods that can facilitate grieving, methods, and approaches that we've lost along the way as our society has become more "civilized," more "developed." Undergirding them all is a collection of studies and assessments from key authorities who have affirmed the importance of dealing with our grief—especially as it affects body, soul, and spirit. I want us to understand that we have permission to mourn those events—deaths, stillbirths, spiritual miscarriages—that have inflicted on our lives silent and agonizing pain.

For our Western culture, this is unexplored territory. Quite frankly, we don't give permission to grieve, or if we do, we tend to grieve badly. In Eastern cultures, there are whole periods of time reserved for grieving, complete with dress code and crowds of people who join with the bereaved to make a whole sobbing party of loss. We could learn much from them. The faith-believing people with whom I grew up are particularly terrible at grieving. We push one another through the process with declarations of "But we have a hope that they have gone to a better place" or "It's all in God's plan!" Yet, even Jesus wept.

What I would like to propose through the discussions in this book is the concept that grief is good. What a strange dichotomy: *good* and *grief*. It confounds our understanding. You may think you are hearing me say that *loss is good*. I'm not. Loss just is. It is a fact of life for a frail and broken humanity. Loss is part of living in an imperfect world—the process of grieving was intended to be the means by which we could shed loss's scaly skin.

There is another thread that runs through this narrative, one that has surprised even me. Dance. Around me is a whole community of dancers who have inadvertently been discovering that our dancing was invaluable in the processing of grief. "Strange ...," you might think. "Why dancing?" This odd juxtaposition of what might seem trivial, frivolous, even irreverent, with something as solemn as loss is puzzling. Channeling mourning through dancing is a bizarre idea—but more typically in our Western culture where we are taught to hold in our grief, not to make it public.

Since I am a dancer and a dance studio director, you might conclude that highlighting dance in this way simply suits my agenda, and you would be right, were I not the sort who typically minimizes the importance of dance as a life essential. Isn't it just for fun? A good pastime? An effective, healthy diversion? It was during my research for this book—which I had initially intended to simply focus on grief—that I found many of the stories consistently included components of dance and, further, that many of the scientific and psychological threads also point to dance as a notable comrade of grief.

Hence, we begin our journey through the lost art of grief-telling, the recovery of solace, and the surprising body-and-soul relief of dance.

2

spiritual miscarriage

*f*or me, my losses were not immediately evident. I had not experienced a major death as Vanessa had. Apart from the death of my grandparents when I was a child and a couple of friends as an adult, I had not really known the depth of grief I had been watching Vanessa go through, and I felt relatively ill-equipped to empathize with her pain. I did know enough, though, to willingly care, constantly listen, continuously comfort.

And then partway through the fall, about a year and a half after Mattea's death, I received a call from an important leader with whom my husband and I had been working on national reconciliation events. It was work into which we had been pouring our lives for the previous ten years. Our commitment resulted in our actually giving up our home, the security of our *normal* lives, finances, and careers to move our family into a motorhome for five years in order to travel the country coast to coast, using the arts (music, dance, storytelling) to convey our message. We had all been *pregnant*, as it were, with hope for change in our nation.

I heard this leader saying to me, "Sandy, we would love to have your arts group as part of this next event, but we would like to request that you, personally, not take part." I could feel a choking in my throat as I held back the tears that were now brimming, unseen by the individual on the other end of the phone. "It is apparent that there is concern about your involvement and I would encourage you to take a step back at this time." I was numb.

A minor comment I had made a year or so previously was at the center of what was now being seen as a serious insult against one of the groups involved in the reconciliation effort. Although the offense was relatively innocuous, its ripple had apparently caused a major reaction. In response, the key leaders had decided to prohibit my involvement in any national activities for the next three years. In other words, in order to maintain peace, I had been barred. When I got off the phone, the sobbing began: uncontrollable heaving and wailing like I had never experienced before. For an hour or so I couldn't speak, breathe, or even get my emotions under control. What in the world ...? When I finally regained my composure, the first person I thought to call, just to process my emotions, was my friend Vanessa. I shared with her the pain, the shame, the hopelessness, the isolation, the dreams that had been dashed, the months—years!—invested, and for what? She broke in immediately. "Sandy, you are describing all of the emotions I have been feeling this last year and a half since the loss of Mattea."

A light went on. Can we truly experience emotional losses in the same way as physical losses? Can we honestly feel a depth of pain over the loss of marriages, relationships, vision, even health, in a way that is comparable to actual death? Some have referred to these as *spiritual miscarriages*. Over the next months and years, Vanessa and I constantly compared notes about our emotions and our process of working through these losses. We discovered that they were consistently, remarkably similar.

What was interesting to me, though, was that although my loss was relatively difficult, it seemed that the depth of its pain was actually rooted elsewhere. I believed that the grief had begun years before I was even born. I sensed that my current pain had piggybacked on an historic one.

Generational grief

My grandparents, immigrants from the Japanese island of Okinawa, had settled in Canada to begin a new life with dreams of peace and prosperity—the twin promises of this new land. My grandfather had accepted the invitation from the Canadian government for internationals to come to help build the Canadian railway in the west. My nana and grandpa were, without a doubt, the most hardworking, generous, and honorable citizens you could imagine. My grandfather had even been risking his life as a *powder monkey*, one of the gutsy men who set the dynamite charges that would blast through the mountains for the rail to be laid.

By 1942, our nation, Canada, was in the thick of World War II and everything was about to change. Fearful for the safety of the nation after the infamous bombing of Pearl Harbor in the USA, the Canadian government had followed the lead of the Americans and determined that all the Japanese in Canada were to be interned, isolated, and/or scrutinized *for the safety* of the country.

My father's family, along with thousands of other Japanese Canadian families, was humiliated. He and so many others had their rights violated—many were expelled from their homes and most had their possessions seized—all in the name of national security. This edict lasted for more than seven years, four years longer than the USA's measures were in place—and the Americans had not seized possessions or properties.

My husband's uncle, also a Japanese Canadian, expressed the agony he felt as a boy when his family was being forced to leave their home and the great dismay they felt at leaving all their belongings (boxed up in their home in anticipation of their return) as they began their voyage to their new internment location, Greenwood, by boat. In a recently discovered letter to his sons, written many years later, he describes his experience:

> In spite of all this my parents built strong boxes to store their china and other valuables. Only to watch the local residents (they could see from the boat) going through the windows of our house taking everything my parents had carefully and painstakingly stored. I hope these people weren't religious persons and believed in another life and the judgement day.

Even my uncle who had just returned from fighting with the Allies in Italy was required, along with all the other Japanese in Canada, to check in with the RCMP every month to ensure that they were not engaged in *suspicious activities*. My uncle was furious at being treated so disrespectfully, especially in light of having just fought for the nation!

Deemed *enemy aliens* in an effort to distinguish them from immigrants who were not from enemy nations, they became the victims of strong ethnic prejudices and were often referred to as *The Japanese Problem*. Growing up, I knew that the experience had left a lasting scar on my dad, on his family's identity, and on their sense of honor as Canadians.

As is the Japanese way, difficulties were never spoken of, they were simply weathered. And so my father's family suppressed their grief and chose instead to prove themselves as trustworthy citizens. They became highly regarded professionals in the fields of medicine, law, education, and the Church, but the sting of their humiliation went unchecked and ungrieved for decades. I believe that it was also unwittingly passed on to the next generation.

Was it therefore possible that my feelings about my current situation, my current rejection, my exile were actually connected to the shame my extended family had experienced all those years ago? Perhaps. More than anything, though, I recognized that my experience had been a *spiritual miscarriage* for me. The very thing that I had been giving birth to—the healing and reconciliation in this nation—had died before it could be delivered. Further, I was being seen as an *enemy*, a hindrance to the purpose our family had been serving these last years.

Why do I call this *spiritual miscarriage*? We nurture hopes and dreams as though we have conceived. They are like a child growing inside us; at the right time, they are meant to be delivered to the world as a gift. When the things we hope for die before they are realized, we can experience it as a death. What is more, like miscarriage, there is no *body* to grieve, and so the loss lingers ungrieved and the pain of the loss persists. These silent agonies can keep us imprisoned, unseen, in a state of perpetual sorrow. But it is grief like any other: it needs to be acknowledged, dealt with, and journeyed through.

Having a funeral

Nineteen years ago, my sister miscarried a baby. The experience left her in a strange emotional plight: she had experienced a loss, but there was no evidence of what had been lost. There was *no body to grieve*. She decided that she needed to honor this lost little life, even though she had only known it in utero. She created a memorial garden in her front yard, complete with a small wooden wishing well that would, for her and her family, be a way to remember the tiny soul that they had not had the chance to know. It has helped in the processing of her grief.

But what about our less tangible losses? How can we begin to process losses of the less bodily sort? My husband, Russ, is a singer-songwriter. He has poured his life into decades of music that have been offered up for national initiatives and a collection of other creative works. He had always dreamed of making an album that would reflect his more artistic desires, and in 2001, he took the leap and began to believe for the possibility of a new music project. Armed with a quiver of fresh songs, and providentially furnished with a topnotch producer, Russ began his creative journey. Thousands of dollars were invested, weeks and eventually months in the studio spent recording, and then, as the final mixes were being completed in Nashville in early September, there was rejoicing. His plan was that on the day following his final day of production, he would take his newly minted album and trek around Nashville, going to the various music executives in this *music Mecca*, and shop his album in hopes of distribution.

He awoke that morning and prepared to meet with label execs, album in hand. But one of the most dreadful events in modern history overtook his plans. He stared at the television in disbelief—shocked by the sickening sight of the World Trade Center's Twin Towers engulfed in smoke, disintegrating floor by floor into the oblivion of the stunned NYC landscape. He halted. There would be no promoting of albums on this day or the other days he was due to remain in Nashville. He had to get home as soon as possible. After the onerous trials of trying to get back to Canada post-9/11, we both understood that our plans to get the album into the hands of music label executives were quite reasonably the least of anyone's concerns.

Any opportunities on this front had understandably evaporated. And we are human. We grieved the tragedy; we grieved on behalf of those who were lost and those they left behind. But we also grieved our lost chance. Our misery deepened as we realized that Russ's songs suddenly sounded full of the most glaringly inappropriate lyrics for those fragile post-9/11 days: "Somethin's rattling, somethin's shakin', somethin' new is goin' down ..."; "Let the oil pour ..."; "Restrain your voice from weeping and your eyes from their tears ..."; "Warriors ..."

In the end, the album got great reviews and gradually trickled out our door through online sales, concert merchant tables, and a small distribution company (which eventually went bankrupt), but the majority of the unnerving stack of CD boxes sat in our garage, year after year, taunting Russ about what might have been. The aggravation of this loss tormented him; fear, anger, jealousy, cynicism, bitterness began to accumulate, and Russ's sense of peace was rapidly dissolving. With the whole world grieving the massive tragedy that was 9/11, what did his little loss matter? And yet he continued to wrestle with deep-seated feelings of failure and disappointment. How could he shake this?

He sensed it immediately: he needed to have a funeral for the album. It might sound strange, but he knew that unless he somehow mourned the loss of this stillborn project, he would remain suspended in grief. And so, on a chilly fall day, he wandered into our damp garage, draped a solitary white sheet over the heap of CD boxes, and bid a sad farewell to his hopes of making a mark with this album ... and he wept ... a physical expression of the deep pain of losing what he had long hoped for and dreamed of.

Soul pain

The foundational feature of spiritual miscarriage is that *what was intended to be* did not materialize. Unaccountably, a tiny thorn of sorrow begins to dig its way into our soul, unsettling and afflicting us with a whole collection of misdirected symptoms.

My friend Susan was born third in a family of four lovely girls—a wonderful, joyful, peaceful family. But there was a disquieting thread tugging discreetly at the fabric of this gentle household that went unnoticed by most around them. By the time my friend was born, the problem had worked its way to the surface, manifesting itself as a serious clinical depression in Susan's mother. Susan grew up in a household that struggled under the constant strain of dealing delicately with her mother, under the suppressed agitations of her father, a household never quite in its equilibrium. For Susan, the whole situation had begun to present itself as a deep, dark, insatiable loneliness.

When she and I began to talk through this lingering despair, it became increasingly evident that this had become a spiritual miscarriage for her. As a child, she had been born into the world with an inherent need for the love and affirmation of her mother, but because of her mother's illness these were rarely forthcoming. The loss had left a conspicuous mark on her soul: regardless of how much affirmation, love, and attention had been poured into her life, this loss had created a hole that was clearly bottomless.

By beginning to process her grief—to weep over the loss of a nurturing mother in her early years; to grieve that her most basic emotional needs had not been met; to mourn that when she had been in despair, there had not been a mother's heart or arms to comfort her—she started to find a sense of release from her pain. As a community of friends around her, we began to reach down to pull her out of her pit of loss. What Susan needed from a loving community of people was caring, crying, affirming, talking, being emotionally available; we were more than happy to oblige. Please note that her mother is one of the most nurturing, loving, joyful, and caring women I know; these were simply difficult years for her.

There are no shortcuts to recovering from spiritual miscarriage. In the same way that the womb must be flushed of any remaining tissue of a miscarried baby, our souls need to be cleansed of the remnants of a painful loss. Any remaining fragments from the loss can actually produce a lingering infection if left unattended. And yet, sometimes, the prospect of purging that object of death is more formidable than living with it.

Tory was a young woman when she began to uncover the memory of her long-term sexual abuse. The perpetrator had been a close family friend, and it took some time for her to uncover the devastating truth about the years when it had taken place. As a protection, her memory had blanked out the reality of the numerous occasions her young self had been violated by this man, but now the memories were beginning to surface—some in her mind, some actually in her body. The anguish that the recovering memories unleashed was unbearable, and she struggled to continue the process of their remembrance. To send them back into the recesses of her subconscious seemed a preferable option, but she could not. Once the keg of recollecting had been tapped, it would not cease its pouring.

This was indeed spiritual miscarriage: the hope of loving and pure family friendships, not to mention the desire to preserve her purity for marriage, had been dashed forever. Again, those around her who did not understand her need to be grieving these devastating experiences misunderstood her emotional disarray. "She's just trying to get attention—she should just get over it!" "Why do you have to keep going through this? Didn't you deal with this already?" And so she would keep trying to push herself through it; keep trying to clean up her messy emotions; keep trying to *rise above* the desire to just flee it all. In and out of the psych ward at the hospital, she worked hard to overcome the torrential pain, going through every therapy, taking every piece of advice, mustering every bit of her internal fortitude—everything she could do she did in an effort to move beyond her current condition, but to no avail.

In the end, she was not victorious. She had called me one day to say, "I think I have figured out how to escape the pain of all this ... it's to be with Jesus ..." Something in me sensed a darkness in this resolution, that it was more than an observation, more than thoughts of peace in years to come. "Yes ... to be with Jesus, but here on this earth—not in Heaven ..." I pressed. "I knew you were going to say that," she responded, "but I really get a sense of peace thinking about being with him *now*." By the end of the week, I had received the shattering news: my friend had taken her life.

Oh ... we had failed her! It was all I could conclude. Had more of us allowed her to just grieve the loss she was encountering rather than judging it and putting expectations on her, perhaps she would have weathered the journey through this valley of shadow.

I have been learning. I have made it my habit to allow the many young women in my midst to sit on my couch and cry for whatever seems to be plaguing them. In my home, in my office, they are welcome to experience whatever emotions happen to be rising to the surface of their emotional sea. Of course, counselors/psychologists are always an excellent source of therapy and care, but I sense that our generation needs so much more. A counselor will not be the friend that is required for the long haul. We need community, long-suffering friendship, unconditional support (I'll cover more of this in the chapter The Gift of Community). Where the counselors in my friend Tory's life were limited was that they could not be her soul mate; as much as they were available, they could not be *there* for her. I could have been ... but in the congestion of my *too busy* life, I found her incessant, seemingly unquenchable, need for care exasperating; at times, even annoying. I am so sorry—I could have made more of an effort; I could have taken more time. I could have ... I could have ...

Guilt came banging on my door, an uninvited, unwelcome—but not unexpected?—visitor, and I found myself battling the sense that I was one of several people who had failed to treat Tory's grief seriously. "One of several"—knowing I was not alone in my failure did not make the guilty knowledge easier to bear. I knew the irritation I had felt when she hit yet another low; I reflected on how I had ignored the many warning signs of her potential suicide ("I know exactly what I would do to take my life ..."); I recognized my own feelings of superiority whenever I was dealing with *her mess*. The guilt of knowing that I could have been more patient, more loving, more understanding, more validating, of knowing that I could possibly have paid more attention to her cries for help, the deep cries from inescapable pain and led to her untimely death, plagued me. I took note.

I am learning to allow spontaneous moments of need to *interfere* with my life. Who knows? That extra hour or two I just spent with someone, giving them the time and the space to pour out the depth of their struggle and pain, may have averted a serious crisis in their life. A spiritual miscarriage is often so difficult to discern or detect. It is only through protracted conversation that a person is able to dissect what is going on internally, to do an *internal examination* as it were. What often comes pouring out is a mixture of what seems rational, what seems nonsensical, and, mostly, what seems like *too much* for such a tiny loss.

With miscarriage, the slightest bit of residual fetal tissue can cause a serious infection. Similarly, grief not properly addressed after a spiritual miscarriage can propagate a progressive affliction of the emotions, and can paint a life with enduring darkness, aching, and anxiety. But perhaps there are ways to change this pattern.

Because so many of the dancers around me frequently cope with the remnants of ungrieved spiritual miscarriages, we have been discovering that dance provides a unique and powerful means by which to extract, to express, these painful emotions. Where there are no words, dance can give voice to the pain and release pent-up emotion. You don't need to be a *dancer*. You simply need to dance. We are all body-soul-spirit beings, so the deep sentiments of our souls are inextricably connected to our bodies. Our emotional health affects our physical health, and our emotions can find release through the movement of our bodies. This frequently overlooked concept can powerfully alter the psychological, physiological, and creative network that is a human being. Its effect can have an impact on two fronts—both for those who express it and those who experience a dance performance—a purging of pain and a cathartic liberation.

3

teach your daughters to wail

i have never been a *crier*. My nana died while I was in junior high school, and when my parents sat my brother, sister, and me down to explain it to us, my siblings were immediately in tears. Me? I sat in silent, somber stillness. "It's okay to cry," prodded my mom. But I remained soundless, there was no emotion forthcoming. Really, not a sense of anything; truly ... nothing. For me, it was a common response to anything painful or sorrowful.

My emotions had always been messy things—in those rare moments when I had dared to permit them the freedom to express themselves, they were intense, angry, bursting storms of vocal eruptions and, by my own judgment, unseemly bawling. It had always been my habit to do everything within my power to keep these humiliating outbursts under wraps. Perhaps it is a habit I developed.

I have an aunt who always talked about my babyhood and about how annoying my cry was. "It always sounded like you had something caught in your throat and you were loud, so-o loud!" I am pretty certain I had no control over how my cry came out, but what I would likely have been aware of, and subsequently learned, was that my cry was inappropriate, it annoyed people. Perhaps it was how I discerned early on that I needed to suppress my crying and keep my intense emotions hidden. But unknown to me, those emotions were all still there, simmering, brewing, waiting for the right moment to burst their banks.

Those bubbling emotions still need a voice, but as my dear friend Sandy expressed when she was dying of rectal cancer, sometimes even what is vocalized is mute:

I am voiceless, and unheard when people try to console me.

It's like they brush off my words and give me new ones. I say, "I don't think I can deal with any more meals right now, or any more dishes that need returning," and they say, "You can just put them in the freezer, and save them for later." I say, "I don't think I want anyone to stay with me at the lodge," and they say, "You'll really like the company." I say, "I'm worried about being at the lodge," and they say, "Everyone at the lodge is so friendly and kind." I say, "I don't want to leave my children," and they say, "Your kids will be just fine."

I feel like I'm in some weird cone of silence screaming at full lung, but no one hears. It gives me such a sense of powerlessness. We say to children all the time, "Use your words," but what if people won't let you use your words? What then? What recourse is there when words aren't enough? When words can't break through? When you're not allowed to say the deep things of your heart? It's hard enough to admit a weakness or a fear, but it's excruciating when people won't accept them. Somehow I'm left with a sense that what I feel is the wrong thing, that I should be able to magically conjure up those words that other people have put into my mouth. So I end up agreeing, and feeling empty of my self.[1]

Her observations are poignant. Grief so rarely has words and our inability to *properly express* our grief can render it inconsequential. What if essential words and emotions are being dropped to the floor? What if tears, one of the key outlets for those emotions, don't come easily? What then?

"Teach your daughters to wail; teach one another to lament" (Jeremiah 9:20).[2] What a strange sort of education. Teaching one another to cry? In my culture, wailing simply does not happen—it is excessive, undignified, embarrassing. People apologize for tears; they dab them away as they well up; they squeeze sobs back into their throats as though they are a sign of failure or of some undesirable blemish on the flawless veneer of our self-restraint. We have become so accustomed to holding them back that, like me, many of us have an inability to allow our emotions, particularly our grief, to emerge in healthy, productive ways.

Ah ... and there is the blockage ... Is grief healthy and productive? In its messy forms—sobbing, anger, wailing, depression, blaming—most of us would argue that it is *not*. So why would we be encouraged to wail? Scroll back a little to our birth. From the second we are born, we know to wail: when we are hungry, when we are uncomfortable, when we are in need, when we are weary. If the slightest thing is out of order in our tiny infant world, we lift up the fullness of our voices to declare to everyone around us, "I AM NOT OKAY!!"

Inappropriate tears

As we get older, our uncontrolled outbursts begin to be tempered by the attentive efforts of diligent parents and those in authority. The eruptions of *I'm not okay!* are delineated by our parents as *anger, demanding, selfishness,* and *actual need.* We duly begin to learn to muffle those surges of emotion that our parents deem inappropriate. We force back angry tears when we are unjustly treated, because a teacher wants us to *play nice*; we suppress the throb in our throats when we have been scorned because an adult wants *peace* and *quiet*; we squelch sobs of grief from loss (a missing toy, a dead pet, a broken promise) because we are told that *big girls don't cry.* A well-meaning adult can indelibly mark the psyche of a young person with comments about the appropriateness, or inappropriateness, of their tears and, ultimately, their grief.

Author and medical doctor Gabor Maté describes honest emotions as a choice we begin to make between *attachment* and *authenticity.* From infancy, our greatest innate drive is for attachment, initially to parents and eventually to other key loved ones. In order to maintain attachment (that is, love and acceptance) with those significant adults, we will often sacrifice our second-most innate drive: authenticity. Maté has observed that we swiftly learn to hide how we actually feel, what we actually think, if we perceive that our true feelings will jeopardize our acceptance by (our attachment to) important others in our lives. Shrouding our emotions quickly becomes an art, an habitual functionality, an evolutionary necessity in order to preserve relationships.[3]

In 7th grade, my group of school friends inexplicably decided that they didn't want me as their friend any longer (yes, relationships in puberty are perplexing). Just like that, I was suddenly cut off from all their activities, phone calls, parties, school-time hangouts, every-thing. Not a single one chose to break from the crowd and stay con-nected with me, so I remained friendless for an entire year. I stayed silent and isolated from everyone, including my family, throughout that painful period. The grief of the experience was mine to be har-bored in mute seclusion.

Years later, my mother confided that she was seriously afraid of what was happening to me internally since there were no tears, no pro-cessing, no speaking of what I was going through. She feared I might do something desperate. It was not until I was in my mid-thirties that this deep and painful memory was reawakened during a coun-seling session and then connected to my inability to establish trust-ing relationships with females. As though I were a 12-year-old again, and the agonizing ordeal had just happened, the tears began to pour out—great, heaving sobs. The heartache of rejection had lingered within me all those years, concealed in the stoic persona of the ma-turing woman. Strangely, miraculously, the tears seemed to bring a swift and immediate healing to the adolescent Sandy.

The wailing women

Tears need to be wept. Physiologically speaking, tears are actually part of a bodily system that helps us to recover after grief (we'll look at this in the chapter The Science of Grief). There seems to be no way around it. It is as though a lid put on a pot of ungrieved tears will only cause them to boil over. Time does not seem to dissipate tears. It appears that the sooner we are able to weep them, the quicker we are able to smooth over their awkward bulge in our being. It's a cu-mulative manifestation of offense, fear, anger, irritation, isolation ...

> "Call for the wailing women to come; send for the most skillful of them." (Jeremiah 9:17)[4]

In 2001, the seventh anniversary of the catastrophic Rwandan geno-cide, we were asked to bring a team of Canadians to minister reconciliation in the nation of Rwanda. In 1994, nearly one million Rwandans were slaughtered by their countrymen over the course of one hundred days. This ethnically fueled massacre had left a nation in a suspended state of grief. With an entire nation grieving, who is there to bring comfort? We began to recruit for our journey. Of the forty team members, twenty were women who all testified that they sensed they were to come and simply weep with the women of Rwanda.

We had no idea what this would mean, but the haze began to clear on the day that seventy-five widows, all victims of the genocide, congregated on the lawn outside the convent that was our temporary African home. "What are they doing here?" I casually questioned our hosts as we were sauntering out from breakfast. "They've come to hear what you have to say." *What we have to say?* My heart was immediately in my throat. Not only were we unprepared for this impromptu gathering, but I also had no idea what we were going to share with these women. A quick "Help, God—what do we do?!" prayer went up from my heart. Immediately, I knew the answer: "Just let them tell their stories."

And so, over the course of an entire morning, we went around the encircled assembly and encouraged all the women, through an interpreter, to give a personal account of what had happened to them and their families during the chaos of those one hundred days. Nothing could have prepared us for the stories we began to hear. "I lost my husband and two children ..."; "I lost my husband and five children ..."; "I lost my entire extended family ... I am the only one left ..." Their narratives included, almost without emotion, horrific tales of running from the killing militia; hiding under dead bodies and in the filth of latrines; seeing children cut down as they ran; watching their families slain before their eyes; being raped by the killers ...

We sat in stunned silence, working hard not to betray our shock at the brutality of the stories. Conversely, shock seemed to be preventing the flow of tears and expression of emotion among some of these mourning women. After we had heard a few dozen stories, one woman, visibly very agitated, finally protested, "Why do we each need to tell our stories? They are all the same!" My response was instantaneous: "Because God cares about what has happened to each of you individually. He cares about each and every particular, painful experience and wants to hear from each of you."

The place of pain

We managed to get more than halfway around the circle of women that first day and determined to continue on for a second day. On day two we awoke to the early gathering of the crowd of women, whose number had doubled to 150. Astonished, we carried on with what had been the program, each woman in turn sharing her story. Halfway around the group on this day, we were again interrupted, this time by an angry outburst from a woman who had been sitting just behind me: "Why have you brought us to the place where our loved ones were slaughtered!?"

"What ... !?" I silently panicked. I looked around to my fellow Canadians, eyes dubious and pleading. "What!?" We would not discover until much later that on the grounds of this convent, six thousand people, many of them family members of these women, had been torched to death while they were holed up in one of the convent's places of worship—given over to the militia by the mother superior and her assistant. "God, why have you brought us here?!" I questioned silently. Again, the consoling response was immediately on my lips: "It is in the place of your pain that there will be healing."

I gazed intently around the circle. Did I truly believe what I was saying? My spirit did, but my mind and my soul were understandably doubtful. How could I, a Canadian from a safe, well-protected suburban life, presume to offer healing for the scorching agony that we had listened to these last days? I had seen the pain etched into their brows as they recounted the violence; I had watched them overcome by shame as they described a rape and the internal damage they had suffered as a result. I had seen the physical scars: one woman's forehead still showed an indentation, the unmistakable result of a beating with a club. Was this really healable?

As each of the stories was recounted, hour after hour for what was eventually three days, we wept for and with the Rwandans. We wept the tears that many of them were still unable to shed, and wept with those who had finally allowed their tears the freedom to overtake them. "Call for the wailing women ..." We were beginning to see the impact of our weeping alongside those who were weeping—an immediate and miraculous transformation seemed to be taking place.

But what was to come next? We all knew that it could only be one thing: forgiveness. Was that even possible in the light of these unthinkable atrocities? We hesitated ... How foolish to think that all this could be blown off with a few words of forgiveness ... And yet, we knew there could only be one way to complete this journey through the valley of grieving, and so we spoke it: "If you want to be free from these perpetrators, you will need to forgive them."

Forgive! Phtt! How I had struggled to forgive those who had stepped on my toes, spoken unkindly about me, rejected me ... What did I know about forgiving murderers? Once more, the answer was promptly before me: "It is the same gift of forgiveness —it has the same power to heal." My hesitation aside, we now led the women in prayers to release those who had slain their loved ones—and a powerful energy began to sweep over the crowd. With great courage and undeniable strength, as though the weeping had softened their resolve, they all began speaking out with forgiveness for the horde of unnamed killers; woman after woman spoke it aloud with confidence and conviction. And we witnessed the impact of forgiveness in the unmistakable transfiguration of their faces as their entire beings were altered.

If that wasn't astounding enough, what happened next took our breath away. All the women, in spontaneous succession, as though mourning clothes had been stripped off them, wordlessly got to their feet, wiped the tears from their faces, and, to the sound of a solitary drum played by one of the women, began to dance—joy now engulfing their frames as they stomped, leaped, and flailed in abandoned euphoria. The unbearable weight of seven years of grief was now lifted. Wailing turned into dancing—an absolute and undeniable miracle!

4

we don't wear black anymore

i am a child of the North American generation that has progressively dismissed the practice of wearing black by the family of a deceased person for a set period of mourning. Black has become a fashion statement rather than a visual declaration of grief—*the little black dress*, *Goth* attire, black formal dress, whatever color is currently popular this season is *the new black*. Historic photos of a plump, dour Queen Victoria, perpetually clad in black in remembrance of her dear departed Albert, have typically perturbed me. It has always seemed overstated and unnecessary—should not the living keep living and show that with color and vitality? Surely black is a superfluous assertion of loss. Shouldn't a person, I have reasoned, just get on with life?

I truly believed that—until late 2008, when my mother very suddenly passed away after a shockingly short bout with cancer. Our brief week of mourning as a family was followed by my swift return to work. Here, my three-week absence to deal with her illness and her passing was being answered with nothing short of a mutiny at my workplace. As dance studio director, I would need to scramble to bring things back into order and my grieving would need to be suppressed. It was an extravagance. There was no time to indulge in my emotions. My sorrow was an inconvenience, and would, by necessity, be forced underground.

No one seemed the least bit aware of, or concerned about, the fact that I was in deep mourning. Showing no regard for my well-being, staff and students launched into angry pronouncements, strong judgments of my weaknesses as a leader, displaying open intolerance for any deficits in my organizational abilities. My emotions were bottled and had been leaking out here and there, but it was clear there would be no understanding, no room for managerial shortfalls. Perhaps if I had been wearing black, reminding my students and staff that I had just experienced a loss—displaying that loss openly—they may have been a little more gracious, perhaps a little more compassionate. But I offered no indication that I might be in need. I didn't cry.

Because we don't wear black anymore, we have lost the medium through which to express, discreetly, our need—our right—to be sad, to shed tears, to withdraw, to be cared for. In generations past, a grieving person could wear black for up to four years. (Queen Victoria wore black from the death of Albert in 1861 until her own death in 1901.) In essence, the whole community would know who was in mourning and would respect their grieving emotions *until the days of mourning were complete*. In our contemporary Western culture, not only is there a lack of acknowledgment of those who are grieving, but there is also a pressure for the mourner to simply *suck it up*, get back to work, take care of the family, get on with life. It's no wonder that so many of us struggle to begin to process our grief.

I have talked with many grieving people who won't even give themselves permission to be needy. They have reasoned, "I don't want to be *one of those people* who demand everyone's attention." These individuals push down the emotions that come bubbling to the surface, never allowing their real pain to be processed. What they have not realized is that, for one thing, they have cast a judgment on those who have been messy, needy, deeming their over-emotionalism to be excessive. For another thing, that judgment has spun back at them, and they have begun to judge themselves as being excessive in one emotion or another and that they must therefore suppress that emotion. This is inevitably unhelpful.

A black signpost

I know of a family who experienced the heartbreaking loss of their baby boy. The siblings, two toddler boys who were just two and three years old, seemed to be only instinctively aware of the sadness that had overtaken their household. And yet, without prodding by anyone, they began to exercise their own version of wearing black.

In that time, their mother began to observe their daily coloring projects. The normally colorful pictures the boys drew were suddenly and almost exclusively replaced by drawings done with black crayons. They offered no explanation. Their aunt observed: "It appeared that these little toddlers were expressing their inner sorrow, their own blackness, in the only tangible way they could—through their creative play."

Months went by, and the practice continued for around six months, when their mother observed that the boys gradually began to incorporate darker-toned colors—browns, hunter greens, and midnight blues—into their drawings. After a few more months, they added dark reds and burnt oranges, new colors but still in the darker range of the color spectrum. According to their aunt, it was "as if their own bodies held a grief calendar. Around the one-year mark after the death of their infant brother, these little boys added the bright colors again—yellow, pink, lime green, sky blue. Their grief had processed and they could again express their creative joy."

But this was not the end of the family's sorrow. Just a year and a half later, the family lost yet another son, a newborn who also died suddenly, unexpectedly. The devastated parents, not knowing how best to weather this fresh wave of grief, recalled their toddlers' reaction to the previous death and decided to *wear black*, but figuratively, in their own manner. The mother opted to demonstrate the severity of her grief by completely shaving her head. It was dramatic and shocking, a cue no one could miss. The father felt the best way for him to show his mourning was to not shave his beard. After months and months of unmitigated growth, he looked like a backwoods hillbilly, which was a conspicuous anomaly in his respectable suburban neighborhood. These demonstrations were a helpful reminder not only for those around them but also for the family themselves so that they could *physically experience* the emotional devastation they were feeling. When the period of grieving was over, the mother grew back and styled her hair, the father shaved his beard, and they moved forward together.

I have a friend who distinctly recalls a similar experience of coloring during a period of great sadness and pain when she was a child. Her pictures also were dark, stark, and angry, and this greatly concerned her mother as each disturbing page of art was completed. Her jovial mother suddenly felt the need to intervene—"Oh, honey, you have so many other colors, see? You can make beautiful pictures"—and proceeded to draw pictures with the brightly colored crayons just to show her. My friend, hurt that her mother wasn't understanding her nonverbal expression of pain, carried this wound, and the associated anger, well into adulthood.

One of the greatest dilemmas when you are grieving, and not wearing black, is that the by-products of grief become so easily misinterpreted. Pain looks like anger; depression looks like aloofness; distress looks like anxiety; anguish looks like discontent. And if grief is just surfacing as anger, aloofness, anxiety, or discontent after a number of years underground, others will often respond with scorn, rather than with compassion.

Power in negative thinking

I have typically been someone who has found it difficult to keep the intensity of my true emotions hidden. But although I constantly suppress my tears, my grieving emotions come out in a multitude of other ways. I generally let the more unpleasant emotions trickle out in not so subtle ways—evasive body language, isolation, intolerance, coolness. These become my protective covering, *my black*. Unfortunately, they don't translate well in relational settings. I become seen as unfriendly, negative, grumpy, antisocial. I tried to explain it to a friend once when she commented on my somber behavior. "I'm grieving," I explained. "There have been a lot of losses recently and I'm still really feeling down." Her response? "But you don't need to be negative all of the time!"

I believe that negative emotions last for as long as they need to. Yes, of course there are times when that negativity lasts longer than necessary due to bitterness and a stunted grieving process, but often *the baby is thrown out with the bathwater* on this front. Dr. Gabor Maté advises that:

In order to heal, it is essential to gather the strength to think negatively. Negative thinking is not a doleful, pessimistic view that masquerades as "realness." Rather, it is the willingness to consider what is not working. What is not in balance? What have I ignored? What is my body saying no to? Without these questions the stress responsible for a lack of balance will remain hidden.[5]

A second hit

The *imbalance* is sorrow that has not been permitted to be expressed or to be adequately processed. For me, it was six months after the loss of my mother that the disregarded grief finally began to churn inside me. I knew it was time for me to address the grief, and so I determined that when the busiest weeks of my work were completed, I would take time away to just go and grieve. I booked three days at a local hotel—all I could afford—and headed off with a friend to let the lid off my pain. Chatting helped; journaling helped more; tears began to leak out. Obviously, it was just a beginning, but I anticipated that there would be some opportunity in the next couple of months for more of the same.

As I was checking out of the hotel that morning, I received an urgent phone call. My youngest daughter, just 12 at the time, was on an island at a school camp and was sick. They were sending her home. My husband had gone away for a work project, so I would need to pick her up. Not a great finish to my days of rest. I had to go immediately to the rendezvous location, an hour's drive away, to meet her and the parent/nurse who had been attending her. The shuttle boat arrived with my barely conscious daughter. She stumbled to the dock deck, staggered to the car, and collapsed into the passenger seat. Less than 20 minutes up the road, she complained about the pain in her back, so I stopped for some ice; another 10 minutes and she was asking if I could take her to the doctor; another 5 and she was demanding that I take her to the hospital. Knowing my daughter was never one to exaggerate her illnesses, I pulled off to the nearest hospital. Half carried, half stumbling, she landed heavily in the seat in the waiting room. My request for the nurses to come and take a look at her was instantly answered with a team of them (all noting my daughter's frightful condition) swooping down to take a sample of her blood (evidently testing the level of her blood sugars), and then swiftly wheeling her now semiconscious body into the emergency room.

Little explanation was given, but everyone was making it evident that we had a crisis on our hands. My daughter, lying insensible and listless, was hooked up to IVs and subjected to multiple tests. DKA (diabetic ketoacidosis) was the conclusion. She needed to be treated quickly before her condition deteriorated further. By late evening her condition had not improved, and the doctor sought to transfer her to the care of specialists at BC Children's Hospital in Vancouver. Two hours later, she was admitted to the ICU at Children's—and swiftly descended into a diabetic coma. Several doctors consulted with one another through the night as her body struggled to cope with a new challenge: her kidneys were failing. Wrestling with a double-edged challenge—bringing her blood sugar to the right level without throwing her kidneys into greater distress—the specialists were confounded throughout her 36-hour coma.

All through the turbulent ordeal, there were healthcare professionals letting me know the reality of her situation: "We had a teen die a couple of weeks ago because her DKA wasn't detected soon enough." Fear was slowly gripping my being. How had this happened? Why hadn't I seen her diabetic symptoms sooner? Guilt was quickly adding to my turmoil. God help us!

Guilt would plague me for the entire time my daughter was in the hospital and for the months that followed. It became the journalist embedded in the war for my peace—a steady stream of internal media coverage on my negligence and failure as a mother. *Flash* the image of her thinner, paler face: I had been too busy at work to book an appointment for her to see the doctor months ago, when I had first noticed her tired countenance. *Flash* the image of her growing listlessness: I was too casually dismissive ("It's probably just an iron deficiency") when others would have dug deeper. The newsfeed from the correspondent in my mind never ceased revealing its condemning evidence of every cue I had missed. The objective voice in my mind was reasoned, sensible: "How could you have known? You don't even know what the symptoms of diabetes are! It's not your fault." It tried to make itself heard, to make me listen. But guilt consistently presented a stronger, louder argument: "It was your responsibility as a mother to pay better attention to your child!" Guilt shouted down reason. I felt consumed by it.

By early morning on the third day, just an hour after I had left my youngest's bedside to nap in the family waiting room, my middle daughter came running in: "She's awake!" The crisis had passed. She was going to be okay, but she would have to stay in the hospital a little longer while the doctors worked to get her kidneys functioning. "She's the only diabetic patient I have ever had to dialyze in the 17 years have been at this hospital!" declared the dialysis technician. We were concerned, to say the least.

For the duration of the next two weeks, while she remained in the hospital, I kept my churning emotions at bay—that is, until a dear friend, Janet, came to visit. "Sandy, I know it feels like it's too much. It's okay to be overwhelmed." With those words, the dam burst and the tears began to flow. This was a woman who was *acquainted with grief*, particularly this sort of grief. Her daughter, Jordan, had virtually lived in this hospital as one medical dilemma after another had challenged this family (see Chapter 13 for Jordan's story). Many friends had come to visit; only this one had come to give me permission to grieve.

I had to grieve that my daughter had been near dying; that I had not detected her illness sooner; that her life would forever be altered; that they could not get on top of the kidney failure; that her diabetes and her kidney conditions required treatments that seemed constantly at odds with one another.

Needing to wrap myself in black

The whole summer, as we struggled to deal with the new regime of carb counting, insulin injections (five shots per day), and balancing the appropriate amounts of each (which seemed the most unbelievably impossible task), I floated between coping and despair. When any new dynamic was added to the picture, my ungrieved fears emerged afresh. When my daughter awoke one morning unable to speak and with an arm that *felt dead* (a temporary condition related to an extremely low blood sugar level and insufficient fuel to the brain), I panicked. When we suddenly discovered that she had developed cataracts less than a year into her illness, I again thrashed myself for my negligence at not having discovered her illness sooner.

Perhaps sackcloth and ashes might have been appropriate at this juncture, as my grief, in the form of self-blame, flogged me. Self-blame partnered seamlessly with my guilt. A partnership made in Hell. "Why didn't you...?" "You should have..." "Because of your failure, she almost died...!" The relentless barrage of questions flooded my brain. I knew the myriad of decisions I had to daily make as a parent—paying adequate attention to my children without making "a big deal" of the concerns I have for them; balancing my family commitments with meeting work deadlines—but this knowledge could not beat back the guilt.

Too much? Too little? It is a difficult balance for any of us to strike. As I allowed myself to accept this truth, I gradually began to release myself from the guilt. Was there really anything I could have done? I drew great comfort from the words of one of the ICU nurses who told me that, "There is a nurse on this ward whose daughter ended up with severe DKA and even as a nurse, she didn't see the symptoms." This thought helped to shake off some of the self-blame, but every day I had to focus determinedly to *not go there* in order to preserve some level of inner peace.

No one around me knew the grip of agony I was in as day after day another wave of grief would strike. As a parent, I knew that it was important to stay strong for my daughter and to not reveal my fear and concern, lest I multiply hers. And yet I now see that had I given her permission for my grief, I would have given permission for hers. Contrary to what we might think, our children are not traumatized by a parent's honest sorrow. Our open weeping, grieving, actually points them toward acceptable and appropriate responses to deep emotion. It is particularly a principle I have learned when counseling those in extreme pain—my empathetic tears will often trigger the pent-up tears of the griever. It would have been wise for me to cry in front of her more often, to cry with her more.

For me as well, the grief from the loss of my mother now mingled with the grief for my daughter but there was no way to express my plight to anyone. I was lonely and isolated; none of it seemed important enough to make it a big deal, and there did not seem to be any room in my relationships for someone like me, someone who was perpetually sad.

I wish now I had had a cloak of black in which to hide myself. The distress and fear kept me bouncing between stoic coping and helpless unraveling. In this contemporary culture, what could be an effective means by which we might be able to cue one another to say, *Take it easy on me, I'm grieving?* Maybe if we reinvented, or re-established the practice of wearing black and created our own symbol of grieving—to wear our version of black, or maybe to color with black crayons for a while—the world around us would appropriately respond to our grief cues.

Ultimately, maybe we need to pay better attention to one another. An observant friend will recognize the signs of the rise of grief: eyes that easily fill with tears, a smile that wavers, a tendency to withdraw. My most valuable conclusion is that the best coping plan is to keep a small group of friends very close and to continually communicate the status of our emotional self to them. A group of friends who are happy to allow the process to take as long as it needs to take. A group of friends who are willing to listen, who don't need to give answers, but can open-heartedly listen. A group of friends who are our caring *community.*

During this time of crisis, I seemed to lose my will to dance. Dance, my passion, my everyday, my living environment was an essential part of me. But the pain of these losses was too acute for me to maintain my sense of self. I was afraid to face the mess of my emotions, afraid to unleash them through movement. Coping had my physical self in lockdown. I could not dance. I was afraid of the pain that might spill out were I to do so. In order to free myself from any condemnation on this front, I had to go back to my understanding of the stages/process of grief to find an explanation for my feelings and my reactions to them.

5

grieving in stages

One of the more unsettling aspects of our Rwandan experience had been seeing the National Genocide Sites. Following the trauma of those one hundred days in 1994, there was a united urgency to ensure that the world, and the nation itself, would not deny that this disaster had occurred. And so, in many locations, rather than clean up—hide—the evidence of the slayings, the bodies were left where they were, in the very positions they had fallen, and sprinkled with lime to preserve them. This had been done so that the grieving nation would be able to step beyond the first stage of grieving: *denial*.

For these grievers to move beyond the shock of their loss, it has been necessary for everyone to accept the reality of the horror of the genocide. It is why the practice of viewing the deceased before they are buried in the ground—as difficult as it is to look at the silent and lifeless figure of a loved one—is ultimately helpful.

Psychologist Elisabeth Kübler-Ross has famously talked about the five stages of grief,[7] what would be commonly understood as *grieving*. I have taken the liberty of looking at what is generally accepted as the journey through grief, suggesting six areas that incorporate Kübler-Ross's five with some common additions:

1. Denial
2. Pain and guilt
3. Anger and blame
4. Bargaining
5. Depression and withdrawal
6. Acceptance and dreaming again

I have observed that a person who is *stuck* at any of these stages of grieving will often become emotionally stalled in this place as well. For example: A person stuck at denial might not have a sense of emotion about their loss, and they may even feel numbed on many emotional fronts for a long period. A person stuck at anger may find their anger piqued by the smallest of circumstances which are completely unrelated to the original loss; an anger with relatively unexplainable reasons. This chapter contains a section dedicated to each of these areas so that we can see how a person might become blocked in their process of mourning at any one of these stages.

Denial

One friend of mine had been stalled at denial for a good five years. At her father's funeral, everyone had complimented her—"She's so strong"—as though her lack of tears was a virtue. Her personality and character saw her slide into the essential role of supporter to counteract the emotional cascade of her mother and sisters, denying her own grief—but for a little too long. More and more, the damaging effects of this obstruction to her grieving were manifesting in surprising ways. Initially, the damage began to show as obsessive-compulsive behavior—locking and unlocking, checking and re-checking the front door before she went to bed each night, even counting the number of times she did so (and sometimes it was hundreds); placing items in their proper place just so, even panicking if they were ever out of order.

Gradually, the damage also became expressed emotionally—anger and fear erupting at an unreasonable level for irrational reasons. During a sharing time with trusted friends, five years later, a sudden and unforeseen surge of grief arose. She began to sob at the memory of her father's passing; she wept over the fact that everyone had complimented her on her strength, which had deepened her belief that she had to keep being strong. The final release of her sorrow brought enormous healing, peace, and rest to her internal tumult.

The ability to accept that a loss has been incurred is often hindered by shock and, residually, denial. Denial is characterized by numbness, a lack of emotional affect, and a general avoidance of the topic of the loss. It will frequently be accompanied by an unwillingness to talk about the person or the incident, as though not talking about it will somehow make the reality of the loss disappear. It is our protective mechanism against the inevitable, and it keeps the overwhelming emotions at bay until we finally feel able to attend to them.

Sometimes this stage of grieving can be extended for those who take on the burden/responsibility of making everything *okay* for the rest of the family, permitting them to grieve while this individual puts their grief on hold. By very virtue of denying their grief, they are in *denial* about how this life-changing loss has altered their life.

Pain and guilt

My friend Tory, who committed suicide, had been opening herself to emotional healing, but the reverberations of her trauma had plunged her into too much despair. Initially, the pain of remembering often kept her emotionally paralyzed for days, but it was the descent of shame, self-condemnation, and guilt that smothered her. "I should have, could have prevented it." "Why wasn't I strong enough, courageous enough, to thwart the attacker?" "I have destroyed my life forever! I will never be clean again!" Tidal waves of pain and guilt were drowning her.

Once the shock of loss lifts, there is often an immediate experience of intense pain; the reality of the loss is now on a collision course with a person's well-being. It is a time when the individual also begins to grapple with the question "What could I have done to prevent this?" A person will comb through their remembrance of situations and circumstances to recall choices, interactions, responses, behaviors that may have averted this calamity. Pain and guilt become the weft and warp in the fabric of sorrow wrapping the victim in intolerable agony.

From here, there seems to be no escape. This part of grief is like the grip of labor pangs: the unstoppable and turbulent, the frenzied and violent; the consuming, smothering agony of pain. There is no liberation; there is only *endurance*, as wave after wave rises and crashes. With labor, breathing becomes the essential coping mechanism; with grieving, it is weeping. When tears are unwept, they literally cause your breath to be held; with the release of tears comes release in breathing. In order to bring comfort during this stage, it is essential to allow the expressions of pain to exist, to be slow to dismiss them. A midwife knows you cannot remove turbulent pain, you can only bring support and comfort as a person weathers the tempest. *Breathe, just breathe through the contractions.*

Thankfully, over time the storm is permitted to rage, the waves diminish, the impenetrable disintegrates, and the calm of day can return.

Anger and blame

A number of years ago, I had been unfairly judged by some important friends in whom I had invested many years. Even worse, some key relationships with others connected to those friends had broken down because of this. Pretty quickly I had forgiven those who had judged me, but in the intervening years I seemed to be unable to break free from the feelings of injustice, and I continued to harbor a sharp sense of animosity toward my friends. I couldn't understand it. Again and again I would speak out forgiveness, offering up the burden of the emotions in prayers to relieve me of this great weight of a broken relationship. One weekend, when I was lamenting again about the situation, suddenly, in a burst of emotion to my husband *(my safe relationship)*, I erupted with, "I HATE what they did to me! Their comments were unjust and untrue! It makes me so mad! I hate that it has affected so many of my relationships!"

Bam! Something in me broke through the wall of enmity, and for the first time in years, my peace returned. Just like that! Why? I believe it was because, very simply, my *anger* needed permission to be expressed. I suspect that I was unable to shed those emotions because my anger was directed at good and loving people *who didn't mean it,* but also because I had no avenue through which I could channel the anger phase of my grief.

This is the toughest stage to embrace, especially if you come from a background like my Canadian one. Canadians endorse the notion that *niceness is good and anger is bad.* As the pariah of our emotions, anger is often deemed an unworthy lodger in the compound of our sane selves. He seems too extreme, too unholy, too uncontrollable—and more than anything, he always seems bent on making a mess. I appreciate Maurice Sendak's classic book *Where the Wild Things Are*[8] for its revealing window onto anger—anger becomes a whole collection of angry monsters over which the boy at the center of the story is made king. The allegory, though relatively *childish* in its construct, is a helpful perspective on our angry emotions. Like beings that insist on having their needs acknowledged, understood, attended to lest they create disarray and chaos, our angry grief needs outlets for expression. Pushed into silence, anger wreaks internal havoc; allowed to vent, it can dissipate.

My friend Stephanie had a similar purging a few years ago. Stephanie has always been one to lavish love and appreciation on any and every leader by whom she has ever had the privilege of being led. As one who has had the privilege of leading Stephanie, I have always known her to be compliant, gracious, supportive, and respectful. Unfortunately, these attributes have played against her at times. Oh, not because there was anything wrong with her respect for these leaders, but because her unquestioning loyalty may have caused some of them to ignore the importance of her heart, her thoughts, her desires. In fact, many of those leaders had treated her as less discerning than them; as less important than others; as though she needed to submit to them for direction and guidance.

This revelation came to her while she was in the process of understanding life and faith on a deeper level. It seemed her emotions had reached an impasse: she did not feel worthy enough or insightful enough. In an instant, her grief began to manifest as an intense anger toward those leaders. Since there had been a strong emphasis on *submission*, she had been required to see the world in the same way as her leaders did—her perspectives, her heart were never factored in. Ultimately, it all caused her to conclude that she needed to be *more spiritual*, that she needed to strive for approval, that she needed to work to line up all her perspectives (which they did not seem to value) with theirs.

She began to process these fierce emotions in a frightful and messy rant in her journal—a shocking piece of prose that she read to a couple of us the next morning. As she delivered her narrative rife with uncharacteristic expletives and furious accusations, we sat riveted. Tears were streaming down my face.

As a dancer, Stephanie chose to translate her newly understood pain into movement. Rather than use music, she created a monologue from the emotional blast in her journal. Angry words became physical (stomping, flailing), her grief expressed by dance of a pedestrian sort (pacing, thrashing), deepening our connection to her tumultuous process and physically unleashing her aching sense of loss—loss of worth, loss of self, loss of care. This honest lament deeply affected us all. Ultimately for Stephanie, it led to a new search for freedom, approval, worth, security in healthy relationships—and trust.

Even when anger slithers into the irrational domain of *blame*, which is also a part of this stage of grieving, it is important to embrace this moment of unreasonableness. However, safe and compassionate friends are a requirement if we are to allow these barbarian sentiments their time at center stage. Those friends must comprehend that this is a temporary state, a temporary reaction to loss. At this juncture we neither want nor need the ineffectual, albeit well-intentioned, dressings of correct thinking, rational solution, or calming of wild seas; these sentiments need to storm, to heave, to blow their hot breath to exhaustion, so that the surging emotions beneath can be liberated. Giving *permission* for them to exist is a large part of the healing and the ability to move beyond this stage.

Bargaining

Murray had lost his first love after years of unresolved and painful relationship breaches. His new girlfriend was the lucky recipient of incessant and, ultimately, frustrating and increasingly obsessive interactions with Murray. He became appeasing, overly compliant, illogically angry, and then, in an instant, outrageously apologetic. Every small disagreement became an enormous emotional crisis for Murray. "Don't leave me!" would be his plea. "You don't like me because I'm a failure," he'd declare time and time again. His entire liturgy of behavior became focused around bargaining with his new love to ensure that she would not leave him—yet he was actually triggering an adverse sentiment because of his fixation on safeguarding himself.

There is a strong association between a loss and the individual's behavior. "Have I done a wrong that is being punished?" "Did I not appreciate the person enough and now they have been taken away?" "Should I have worked harder to have prevented the loss (of the job, of the marriage, of the business)?" These become the bargaining chips: "If I just _____ (behave better, work harder), would you please _____ (heal, restore, bring back ...)?"

Once the effects of the loss begin to be unearthed, there is frequently a longing to make the pain go away; an aching desire to alleviate the intensity of the loss by an agreement with the unseen *powers that be*. In this phase, our emotions swing toward the non-negotiable possibility of changing the course of history, a longing to remove this terrible outcome that cannot be undone.

Depression and withdrawal

As a young girl, Sandra had suffered traumatic emotional abuse at the hands of an older brother. Fear, terror, and depression plagued her throughout her life as a result of this wounding. The depth of her pain went underground, rising and falling symptomatically as depression until she was well into her thirties. She chronicles the process of unpacking this pain in her book *Passionate Embrace – Faith, Flesh and Tango*.[9]

At times her depression would have her locked away in seclusion under the dark heaviness of its shroud with little light, little hope. But over the years, as she has been addressing her emotional angst, she has discovered some helpful tools to lift her beyond this point. It was specifically her unique experience with learning the *tango* that brought her an exceptionally profound release from the weight of her depression.

A doctor friend of mine told me that more than 80% of her patients are struggling with stress, anxiety, and depression. She actually prescribes more antidepressants and anti-anxiety drugs than any other pharmaceutical. In our contemporary Western culture, we are more inclined to medicate, rather than process, suppressed inconvenient emotion. Depression specifically is frequently overlooked until it becomes acute. We mistakenly dismiss its underlying causes because it looks too much like *negativity*. In this stage, an individual is often encouraged to think positively or to *just get over it*. It is the *just getting over it* that pushes a person to circumnavigate around depression, pushing its damaging emotional and relational effects underground.

I once had a teacher who would always refer to the word "therefore" as being a key in a discussion. "Whenever you are reading something," he would say, "and you come to a 'therefore,' you need to pause and find out what it is *there for*." I feel as though we need to add a "therefore" before depression. In this way we might pause after "therefore depression ..." and find out what it is *there for*. I believe there are crucial things that might be uncovered if we were to take a look at what might be precipitating our depression. What pain is still ungrieved? What loss has not been addressed? What wrong is being done to us? What cruel behavior is being inflicted? What abuse or grief of another are we carrying with us?

Acceptance and dreaming again

One of the most compelling aspects of the Rwandan recovery from grief is that Rwandans have a deep sense of hope and vision for their nation. They have fully embraced what they did to one another during the genocide, have repented and reconciled, and have begun to rebuild their nation in every way. Some have even dared to stand side-by-side with hated enemies. No longer permitted to talk about whether they are Hutu or Tutsi, the Rwandans are courageously launching into a new day for their beautiful nation. They even have a strong sense that they will become a powerful voice for reconciliation, helping to bring healing to other nations.

They are caring for one another's orphans (with so many adults dead, there are countless children left parentless). You have never seen such a staggering number of well-behaved street children wandering a city.

We even heard the story of a woman whose son had been murdered by a young man. The murderer's mother made the long trek to the home of the dead boy's mother in order to apologize for the wrong her son had done. The grieving woman, moved by this humble act, accepted the woman into her home and forgave her for her son's misdeeds. Not only that, but when the rest of the townspeople discovered that the murderer's mother was in her home and threatened to kill her, the grieving mother brought the woman into her bed with her for the night, so that she would be safe. This was undeniable evidence of true forgiveness and a profound acceptance of the loss.

Our dancing Rwandan widows were also exhibiting their acceptance when they began to dance. To finally accept the scope, the magnitude, of the loss, to embrace its consequence, is to reach the denouement of grief. It is by no means the end of the pain, the longing, the desire for the return of what has been lost, but it does signify the beginning of a desire to dream again. To dare to hope that extending forgiveness to an enemy can result in peace. To dare to believe that another pregnancy will not necessarily end in miscarriage. To dare to envision another project that will be accomplished. To dare to trust that another relationship might end well.

Many pause here and reason, "Surely if I don't bother to take a risk again, I will prevent any further pain." Individuals become locked into surviving and so cease thriving. If bitterness has taken root, it is even more unlikely that a person will move forward into this redemptive step of acceptance.

Although there is no guarantee that *all* will go well from this point on, or that the memories of the past will not provoke a familiar ache, even years after, there is some level of hope. The return of hope is often accompanied by a maturing of outlook, a tenacity of effort, and a deepening of character—all a strange and perplexing outcome for what had seemed so damaging.

It is worth finishing here with a reassuring quote from Elisabeth Kübler-Ross:

The most beautiful people we have known are those who

have known defeat, known suffering, known struggle, known loss, and have found their way out of the depths. These persons have an appreciation, a sensitivity, and an understanding of life that fills them with compassion, gentleness, and a deep loving concern. Beautiful people do not just happen.[10]

6

dancing

I t begins as a slow jazz lament—strains of "Just a Closer Walk with Thee" swung with a soulful blast from trumpets, trombones, and tubas as the mourners begin to file out of the church. An energetic woman in a brightly colored dress, a matching umbrella in hand, begins to strut rhythmically down the street. Following her is a second woman, also vibrantly dressed but even more flamboyant, her umbrella decorated to indicate that she is leading the dance. She now steps out in front of the crowd with dramatic exuberance and picks up the rhythm of the steps, guides the procession from the church door to the pavement.

Halfway down the street, as though the right moment has come, the instruments stop and a lone drum introduces a new, faster tempo. Now the first woman blows a whistle, and suddenly the musicians strike up a lively Dixieland version of "When the Saints Go Marching In," the brass wailing and blasting, and the whole assembly begins to let loose with dance. Friends and family abandon themselves to the melody and rhythm, unleashing a full-blown celebration. Remarkably, a casket appears in the procession. The pallbearers lift it high overhead and then lower it, beginning to pick up the rhythm with the coffin. Swaying in time with the music, they lift and lower it again, bobbing it to the beat.

Lamentation and restoration

What the mourners of New Orleans have discovered is an effective remedy for the sorrow that ails them. This unusual observance is a brilliant fusion of lamentation and restoration: in part a release of arrested grief, in part an unleashing of therapeutic mechanisms. As mentioned earlier, grief settles in the body and requires a physical outlet.

Many cultures around the world have similar practices. The Pakistanis use the rapid tap of traditional drums and whining melodies of traditional flutes to stir the mourners into dancing. In Ghana, pallbearers don matching suits and do a choreographed dance with the casket precariously perched on their shoulders—even lowering themselves to their knees while still bouncing and swaying to an African beat on an amplified Casio keyboard. In New Zealand, a Maori haka is part of the mourning ritual—a powerful chant with warriors simultaneously performing forceful, meaningful gestures—a rhythmic slapping of the thighs and chest, a wave of the hands side to side, an authoritative stomping of the feet, a pounding of the air with the fists—and calling out in unison their fierce, passionate cry for the lost warrior.

What all of these have in common is a sense of an unleashing of the suppressed emotions—a cry, a wail, a stomping and whirling, a letting loose of the body to release its sorrow. It is a cathartic endeavor to alleviate the emotional pain of the loss. They have intuitively understood the need to trigger the body's natural pain relief responses, in particular, those invaluable endorphins that are inhibited by the crisis of grief.

In many cultures, somehow grief becomes a whole-body expression. A Haitian woman might pour out her lament in a dance before the coffin of her dearly departed, but this type of response is foreign to my culture. This was why, on the morning after Vanessa delivered her precious Mattea, when she had called with an urgent request that I come over to her home, I was taken aback by her pronouncement: "I feel like I was inspired to create an entire dance production based on this loss."

Of course, I had been with her the day before and held the tiny lifeless body and knew I needed to be—wanted to be—there for whatever she needed. But I was baffled when I arrived at her place and she filled in more of the details: "Sandy, my husband is going to think I'm crazy, so I need to tell you what I've been up all night doing." Over the next hour, she poured out to me all the precise details of the dances, the dancers, the themes, the styles, the backdrops, everything for a full-length dance production. She was as astonished by it all as I was.

Why would a normal woman in the throes of extreme grief turn to dancing as an outlet to her pain? What is it about dancing that makes it a partner to grief? Yes, the physical exertion releases endorphins, which make a person feel good, but so does a good run. What does dance offer that other physical exertions do not? I would suggest the following:

1. It gives a voice to grief
2. It releases the pain of grief
3. It provides a means to respond to grief
4. It aids recovery from grief

A voice

It has been said that "a picture is worth a thousand words." Dance is essentially a series of moving pictures; where words prove inadequate for the expression of the innumerable emotions that surface after loss, dance can become their wordless expression. As Gilbert and Sullivan expressed through Katisha in their famous opera *The Mikado*, "Your body is the voice that sings what there are no words for, the instrument that plays the music of your soul."[11]

Dance can even express utterances beyond conscious comprehension. Author Madeleine L'Engle observed this about art, saying:

> I did not understand it but I knew what it was about. As long as we know what it is about, we can have the courage to go wherever we're asked to go, even if we fear that the road may take us through danger or pain.[12]

So many of the emotions resulting from loss cannot be understood by our conscious minds, but a creative expression like dance (or any other art form) can permit us to go to difficult places in the articulation of our pain, extending beyond what the mind can decipher in its foggy, grief-inebriated state.

As I sat with Vanessa the day she had poured out her dance vision, she began to acknowledge the emotions associated with her grief. She recognized that the first of her responses to her baby's death had been shock. When we are in shock, reality becomes nonsensical—conversation cannot be comprehended and sound is dulled, as though an explosion has gone off too close. Peripheral awareness becomes heightened, we become sensitive to minute details—the tick of a clock, the beep of a medical machine, the pasty color of the hospital walls—and all words seem to escape utterance as though the victim has become mute.

Vanessa's first dance piece was to be choreographed to the sounds of a voice message from hospital staff informing her that her baby had died; the beep, beep, beep, bee~p, of the heart monitor; the blank faces of stunned onlookers—all evoking for her (and eventually for the audience) the traumatic news of the unfathomable.

An expressionless dancer enters the space, the evidence of shock can be seen in her small, slow, pained steps; the ache of her being in the strained contraction of her torso; the feeble enfolding of her arms. A hollow look of powerlessness accompanies the steady pacing and aimless, indecisive stumbling of the feet round and round the empty stage.

There are dozens of numb, dumb emotions during the grieving process that simply have no words. Those around the bereaved often press them: "Just tell me how you are feeling, so I can help you, care for you." A wordless response will, more often than not, produce a deceptive sense in those others that they are *off the hook* because "she just *didn't let me in*." But, *there are no words*.

Although most of us would say that we are not dancers, and would therefore never *dance out* our grief, it is helpful to know that much of what we are going through will not have words and that there is a need in our being to express, in some way, our reactions to those moments that render us speechless. Art of all sorts—from writing, to theater, to film, to music—can assist in conveying volumes of mute despair. There is a unique added component in dance, as we will discover throughout this book, that enables not only the soul (emotions) and mind/verbal connection, but also the body, which has a whole other series of ramifications for grief's impact on the physical being.

Releasing the pain

Vanessa's second response was even more difficult to convey: *panic*. How does one begin to communicate that, were it not for their skin, their entire being would be running in a thousand crazed directions—nowhere to hide, nowhere to find peace, nowhere to ease the pain? Half a dozen dancers running in dozens of directions—expressions of pain, alternating with self-comfort and interspersed with arms splayed in desperate, voiceless cries of resignation—all became the words that uncorked the bottled chaos she felt.

The pain of grief implants itself in our bodies. In our dance studio, we have created an open and safe place where dancers are free to allow the releasing of whatever emotions begin to emerge during class. It is contrary to what you will most often find in other dance studios, where young dancers are encouraged to *leave their emotions outside the classroom*. Many times I have watched as a dancer in my studio begins her barre exercises and the tears begin to flow. "What's going on?" the instructor will ask. "I have no idea," is generally the first response. But as the individual assesses her feelings, her responses, she will discover that her dance had begun to unlock memories of pain (an abuse, a rejection, a loss).

Suppressing the components of our pain on the physiological level also suppresses many vital bodily functions. Dr. Gabor Maté has commented in his lectures on how emotional stress affects the body[13] that children who tell no one about their sexual abuse, and then need to repress the emotions related to that abuse, cause long-term physical and emotional harm to themselves. Especially for a child, how can those words begin to be expressed in a safe place? Dance-movement therapy is an effective psychotherapeutic strategy based on the belief that mind, body, and soul are inseparable. It has been an effective approach, particularly with children, to begin to release the pain of their grief in nonverbal ways.

Responding to grief

Vanessa continued to translate her grief into dance. Every stage of the grieving journey on which she was about to embark had a place in her dance production. The calculating and assessing of all that had gone wrong with the pregnancy was imagined as a dancer studying and analyzing a stage full of criss-crossing chalk lines. The struggle to find comfort became a duet of dancers, one rolling toward and then away from the other, the other pursuing the first in an effort to provide solace.

Ultimately, as an individual journeys through grief, there is a desire to look for connections that can restore the will to live. Relationships, evaluating, moving forward all become difficult, but are necessary tactics in the processing of grief. *Life* and *expressions of life* become essential to embracing vitality rather than hopelessness.

The *life* expressed through dance has been noted by Henry Havelock Ellis (physician, psychologist, writer, and social reformer of the 1850s–1900s) who declared that "Dancing is the loftiest, the most moving, the most beautiful of the arts. For it is no mere translation or abstraction of life. It is life itself."[14]

And dancer/choreographer Martha Graham once said to fellow dancer Agnes de Mille:

> There is a vitality, a life force, an energy, a quickening, that is translated through you into action, and because there is only one of you in all time, this expression is unique. And if you block it, it will never exist through any other medium and will be lost.[15]

There is a sense of hope that is instilled through a moving body—it is an affirmation that life continues, that all is not lost, that our existence means something to the world around us.

Recovering from grief

At a turning point in Vanessa's dance production, a young girl enters the scene: she looks at, touches, and then quietly sits down beside the lead dancer. It is a peaceful and moving moment in what has, to that point, been a tumultuous journey. One of my friends who attended the production is a native of Rwanda and lost many of his family members in the genocide. When I asked him what he thought of the production, his main comment was about the young girl: "She was obviously a sign of hope and comfort—that after all of the loss, there would be something young, new, that would restore hope."

On both an emotional level and a physiological level, the *creative* dimension of dance allows it to have an even greater impact than any other physical activity. We will address this more deeply in Chapter 11, The Science of Grief, but for now let us turn to renowned Romanian biologist and physician Ana Aslan, who has noted a physiological connection to creativity. Norman Cousins speaks of her in his book *Anatomy of an Illness*: "She [Ana Aslan] is convinced that creativity—one aspect of the will to live—produces viral brain impulses that stimulate the pituitary gland, triggering effects on the pineal gland [which stimulates rest and a sense of well-being] and the whole of the endocrine system [which maintains homeostasis]."[16]

Strikingly therefore, in addition to the physical benefits of dance, its creative aspects also aid in the restoration of the body after crisis. The very nature of dance in its creative capacity can actually produce new neural pathways, which inevitably facilitate the body's drive toward life and cognitive health. And further, endorphins, which are released during dancing, restore a sense of the joy of living, and release the effects of depression and hopelessness that are frequent cast members in grief's theatrics.

Beauty

I add one more component to this list of dance's impact on a grieving life: it restores *beauty*. Death exacts its effect in our souls with dual impact. We are both haunted by the cruelty of death and prompted to remind ourselves of the treasure that this life, now departed, was to us. It is a moment to reflect on the gift of life, the relationship with the lives around us, and the undeniable blessing of the beautiful world in which we live.

> Beauty feeds the soul; it lifts the spirit and it inspires positive thoughts and feelings. What food is to the body, beauty is to the soul.
> (Eleanor Cardozo, bronze artist)[17]

There is an essence to living, a vitality that is generated by the beauty of the dance form. There is something in the impact of beauty that brings life out of death. It is an inexplicable illumination, a light in the bleakness of a grieving soul. In the months that followed the loss of Mattea, Vanessa had gone to an ocean-side resort to rest and be restored, and it was here that the vision of her final dance came. She stood on the shore as patient wave after patient wave began to wash the shore. She marveled at the beauty of the flow of water; the beauty of the dampness smoothing clean the sand; the beauty of the calming, repetitive lapping; the beauty of the endless sea.

These images were mimicked by Vanessa's dancers gently side-rolling in alternating sequence along the width of the stage, the lead dancer now walking serenely through the *waves*, stroking her face and swaying in peaceful, hopeful resolve. The storm had been weathered and the calm had come. Through our profound experience with Vanessa's grief, we came to understand that as Tolstoy said, "Art is not a pleasure, a solace, or an amusement; art is a great matter. Art is an organ of human life, transmitting man's reasonable perception into feeling."[18]

Grateful for the release of these pent-up, unspent emotions, Vanessa recognized that her dance journey was her effective vehicle in which to convey her departed baby to a place of rest in her aching soul. And further, the group of dancers with whom she had embarked on this creative journey into pain became a uniquely caring community that wrapped itself around her in her time of greatest need. The unexpected gift of community was another important key in our understanding of grieving well.

7

the gift of community

Lydia almost died when she was born. Her life seems to have been death-defying ever since. Her mom was broken, having been abused for most of her life, so it was understandable that her manner of dealing with her children had the same damaging flavor as her early care. Subsequently, Lydia was regularly verbally abused, ill-treated, and physically knocked around by her mother's out-of-control rage. Her father was broken too, but his anger was a quietly boiling sort. It exploded less frequently, but when it did, it spewed out scalding lava and inflicted emotional third-degree burns.

In her early pubescent years, Lydia was sexually abused by her brother's friends. Her shame and mortification remained under wraps for years due to the lack of a trustworthy confidante of any description. And if that weren't enough, when she was only 14, her father announced that he was gay and was leaving her mother. The family broke apart, divorce was imminent. In her small northern town, her school counselors advised that she keep this *scandalous* occurrence a secret. Her emotional needs were entirely ignored.

In addition to all these painful factors, or perhaps because of them, Lydia remained friendless throughout high school. Beside the pop machine in the bustling high school hallway, she would sit through a friendless lunch. Alone. Painfully alone. Head down, unseen, unseeing. The solitude gripping her became a gnawing, angry, bottomless hunger that gave birth to her daily companions: anguish and despair.

The agony of the multiple losses, humiliations, and abuses had morphed into an intense and temperamental demeanor that seemed to attract further abuses, rejections, and isolation for this heartbroken young woman. There were no words for this level of grief.

But one unlikely diversion found its place in her shattered life, a single, albeit slight, glimmer of hope. Dance. Instructors might berate her, students might scorn her, multiple times she might be told she had neither the talent nor the body type, but in the midst of the tumult, she would find an almost imperceptible breath, one only her soul could detect.

And it was her soul that led her deeper, further into this strange camaraderie. Expression borne of physical lament; intensity released from contained pain; exuberance springing from relief—all became a language for words that could not be spoken, for grief and pain that could not be verbalized. Hand in hand with her partner, dance, her pain found its voice. It found its translator, its advocate, its confidante. In dance, she had control. She could push herself to accomplish more, to be stronger, to create what she wanted, to say what she had never been permitted to say, to physically lash out and hammer at her invisible tormentors.

Unexpectedly, she found an added gift in the dance studio: the care of a loving community of dancers. Here she began to share her story —grief-telling and dancing her way through some of the most painful details of her life experience. The steely edges of her character, so often misunderstood by others, began to be gently molded and softened by the constant love and compassion of one or another of her companions. As she danced and shared, the remnants of her harrowing history began to be expelled. At times the pain has been too overwhelming, or the fear of another rejection too forbidding, and she has pulled away, but again and again, her dance community has offered her refuge and constancy.

Enough time

It was by accident that we discovered the invaluable gift of community. Where previous generations lived in each other's pockets, concerning themselves with each other's livelihoods, social prospects, familial destinies, and emotional states, our current culture is disturbingly uninvolved. It has increasingly abandoned community as a human essential, leaving many isolated and alone. Around our household and studio, we have had the privilege of rediscovering its gift.

Of course, social media helps us maintain a pseudo sense of connection with one another, but were I to close my computer, it would be a rare Facebook friend who would materialize at the door of my home to see how I was doing. A lamenting Tweet will not likely send comforters running. Albert Einstein said, "It has become appallingly obvious that our technology has exceeded our humanity." What would he think of us now?

We have not only become solitary, we have also become miserly about sharing our time, our relationships, our resources, our selves. We divvy up the hours of our day between the demands of work, our exercise regimes, our family time, and our social calendars in such a thorough way that we are inclined to become agitated, even annoyed if another's need spoils its orderly parameters. It is too easy to brush another's need away with a curt, "I've really got too much on my plate right now ..."

Caring for others tends to be the first cut when we review our personal time budget. It does not necessarily fulfill the goals of my ambition; it will not pave the way for my success; it takes away from my own depleted emotional resources. It is an imposition in every way. To some of us, it is an inconvenience from which we unashamedly run. We have become experts in maintaining a grand scope of friendships and amateurs in genuine intimacy and care. Unwittingly, we have sacrificed everything on the altar of self-sufficiency—only to discover that we have sold our souls to isolation.

For me, community is about sharing my life: allowing the chaos of another's circumstances to infringe on mine; permitting myself to be known without constraint; resigning myself to needing others. I would suggest that we could better deal with the onslaught of grief and loss (and their debilitating effects) if we could better share our lives. Even though our society has assembled an excellent collection of psychologists and counselors, they will never be enough to stem the plague of emotional destitution.

The suicide of my friend Tory was immediately followed by that of another friend, Justine, who hanged herself while on leave from a psych hospital. A few years later, Kelly followed suit. She, like the others, took her life because of an inability to escape her despair. Of course, suicidal depression involves a complex set of dynamics. I know that answers to an individual's torment at the hands of this incapacitating ailment are not simple, but I also know that each one of those women died feeling the same anguish—they felt alone, entirely alone. Yes, of course there were other individuals in their lives, but there was never enough consistent care from those loving persons to counteract the depth of their anguish.

I am quite convinced that a community could have answered their call. That bottomless pit of grief is usually simply too much for single individuals to begin to deal with, but like a great physical burden resting on the shoulders of one or two people, that same weight becomes effortless when borne on the shoulders of many. Sadly, psychiatric institutions—where loved ones come for brief and cordial visits; where patients can lose their sense of identity; where life can become purposeless and unwinnable—can reinforce the sense of isolation, often intensifying the misery.

When those same individuals are placed in a community where they can contribute, no matter what stage they are in, they can find nuggets of hope that can sustain them through the darkness of depression. A collection of relationships with which they are able to spontaneously connect when despair hits, and where they can sort through the pain before it completely overwhelms them, is an invaluable alternative.

Let's get talking

Often the greatest need is to be able to talk about all that is going through the mind of a grieving person. Emotional illness can be the extreme result of unvoiced need. My friend Kaitlin was in the throes of the difficult birthing of her third child—a huge baby boy who was nineteen days overdue—when the doctor commented, "You're a little girl and this is a huge baby. You're going to have trouble no matter what I do." Regrettably, he did not make a note of his own observations.

As labor progressed, she could feel that something was terribly wrong. Alarmed, she exclaimed this to her doctor and husband, who were sitting chatting, oblivious to her plight. The two men turned and looked, unmoved by her cry. "It's just how labor goes," the doctor commented pragmatically to her husband. Her turmoil was just white noise to their conversation.

This was her third delivery. She knew perfectly well "how labor goes," and she knew that this time something was amiss. Again, she pleaded, "No, I really think you need to help me!" They again turned and nodded indifferently, as though reluctantly appeasing a demanding child. In that moment she had a consuming thought: "If I had a gun, I would kill myself right now." She spoke this thought to the nurse, but the dismissive response was simply, "It's always bad."

Another few moments, and panic began to course through Kaitlin's being—she felt life begin to drain from, and death begin to overtake, her faculties. "Help ..." she muttered, her voice trailing, doubtful that there would be any response.

She doesn't know whether they eventually heard her or whether they suddenly saw her in trouble, but the doctor awoke to her plight and began doing a quick internal check. "Oh dear, this baby is about to send both mother and baby into distress! We need to get him out right away!" A high forceps delivery finally removed this whopping 10-pound baby from his mother's tiny frame, brutally tearing her in the process. She was lauded as a hero—"Look at the size of him!"— but felt betrayed—"You're all idiots! I told you there was something wrong and no one was listening!"

The crisis left its mark. She had been dying and no one would help her. But her torment had to be pressed underground, superseded by the urgent needs of a newborn and the constant demands of her other two children and her household. She struggled to feel love for her new baby, she felt no joy, no desire to even keep him. Her husband, unwilling to share the load of nighttime feedings, requested she let him sleep, and so she would get up to feed and change the baby on her own. She remembers frequently laying the baby on a blanket on the floor so that she could clean up the blood that had dripped everywhere around the house. Blood? Hers. A continual leakage from the internal damage of the high forceps delivery.

For two years she would be unable to talk about the anguish she silently suffered, its rising torrent daily threatening to drown her. For the most part she would not notice the creeping tide. She was the personality type that had to be there for everyone. She was highly conscientious and capable, but the impact of her unaddressed grief would soon overcome her. It arrived in the form of a severe postpartum depression two years after the original trauma. For months, years, she would struggle to cope with her own needs, not to mention the daily needs of her family.

In Anita Diamant's acclaimed novel *The Red Tent*[20] she details the cultural experiences of the ancient Jewish desert dwellers who assigned a tent in which the women of the community would gather for all life events from delivering babies to coaching young women through life changes (even menstruation was apparently a time for gathering), to caring for one another and one another's children, to grieving together. In these communal times, a woman could talk through a traumatic birthing experience, or receive advice on a difficult marriage, or be emotionally carried by the others. I often wonder, if Kaitlin had had a red tent to go to, a community of women with whom she might have been able to talk through her trauma, perhaps the trial of the long journey out of her depression may have been averted.

I remember this from the trauma of my own childbirths. Yes, true, most women will never talk about childbirth as trauma, but for many—those who experience long labors, or excruciatingly painful deliveries, or life-threatening circumstances—there is an added dimension of distress in the recovery from childbirth. Like hunters and warriors telling their tales, women have a similar need to unpack, to talk about, their life-changing experiences in order to alleviate the pain of the trauma.

I have often found myself walking again and again through the memory of one or another of my birthing experiences, making note of the unusual grip of agony as the baby got stuck and labor was not progressing. Of contraction upon contraction with no rest between them and no respite from the pain. Of grabbing the collar of my doctor, as I was wheeled into surgery for an emergency cesarean section, growling in desperation like some deranged animal, "You've got to give me something for this pain!" Of my family, standing at the end of the hallway, grinning and waving happily as I passed by. The strange juxtaposition of my dread with my family's joy has always perplexed me.

It has been as though I am driven to talk about it over and over, just to lessen the dismay I felt, and perhaps continue to feel. I recall the shock-infused silence between my husband and me as we sat in the recovery room after the extraordinary agony of my second child's birth (also stuck). It was as though we had just faced death and been rendered mute. For some reason, we sat stunned, nursing a sense of *no one else in the world will be able to relate to what we have just gone through.* We had no means to express what the experience had done to our emotions. It has only been in the years since that I have been able to bring a sense of peace to the remembrance by talking it through.

I don't think that any of the mature women in my life ever spoke of childbirth when I was growing up. My mother always said that it was "not too bad," but I then discovered that she was of the generation who were systematically given epidurals (or expediently booked c-sections) and tidily positioned on their backs with their feet in stirrups for the convenience of the doctors. They labored solely in the presence of medical personnel, without the consoling presence of the father. I think my dad was at home watching a football game during my birth. Childbirth was neatly packaged as a quick, painless, impersonal little blip on the life meter. Understandably, I had not been prepared for the reality.

What community can look like

In generations past, smaller, tighter-knit communities provided a generous amount of social support. A woman's connection to her local community was how she was able to survive postpartum, deal with financial challenges, cope with a house full of children, manage on her own when her husband was no more. Meals were brought to the door after the birth of a baby or the loss of a loved one. Shared childcare, either by relatives or by neighbors, not only alleviated the pressure for moms to be continuously *on duty*, but also enhanced the socializing and relational maturity of the children. Teenagers and young women were able to process the upheaval of life changes and relationships with older women whose life experience gave them understanding and wisdom.

In our culture today, women have, in the words of nutrition specialist and author of *Rushing Woman's Syndrome* Dr. Libby Weaver, "taken on jobs like our fathers while still maintaining the responsibilities of our mothers."[21] The stresses and pressures of our fathers' lives are now being carried by working women—but the family responsibilities have not been removed to make space for the new responsibilities. There is an expectation that a woman should be an ambitious career woman, a business aficionado who also creates and maintains the perfect home, complete with tasteful interior design, gourmet meals, and handcrafted detailing, all while caring for and meeting the needs of the family, staying fit, and engaging in interesting hobbies. With so many demands on our time, the emotional disturbances of life have become a notable inconvenience. Most of us have tragically chosen to live by the creed of *suck it up, princess*, presuming that to ignore the things that cause us pain and grief is a demonstration of strength, honor, and courage. Regrettably, inevitably, we are suffering for it.

In addition to the loss of community, women now carry a heavier burden of external stressors, and it is becoming apparent that our physical health is being affected in ways never before observed. Increased levels of stress combined with a decrease in social support are having a disastrous impact on us. In a study of 514 women who required a breast biopsy, led by psycho-oncology expert Dr. Melanie Price from the University of Sydney, researchers set out to discover if stress was a key factor in the development of breast cancer. They gave each woman a "Life Events and Difficulties" questionnaire and uncovered something unexpected:

The crucial factor in this model is not the stressor, but the

complex interaction between stressors, personality, and social support that affect an individual's ability to cope ...
Women should be reassured that stress per se does not
cause breast carcinoma (cancer); however, in the *absence
of intimate emotional support* [emphasis mine], situations of
severe stress may increase a woman's vulnerability to this
disease.

The researchers strikingly concluded that:

Women experiencing a stressor objectively rated as *highly
threatening* and who were without intimate emotional social
support had *a ninefold increase in risk of developing breast carcinoma (cancer)* [emphasis mine].[22]

Notably, there is even a natural process in our physical makeup that
encourages us to seek out social support. If we look into our physiological response to stress and grief we find that stress naturally
releases *oxytocin*, the hormone that stimulates the desire for a hug or
for social support. This hormone can even generate heart cells, heal
the body from stress-related damage, and protect our whole cardio-
vascular system during grief. Remarkably, the more we reach out for
support, the more oxytocin is released, and the quicker the recovery
from stress and grief.[23][24]

Practical community

The emotional social support around my life, the community, has
chosen to be honest and vulnerable. We get *bare* with one another.
When we ask, "How are you doing?" we aren't just being polite, we
are looking for an honest response. "Not good," will most often provoke a request for more information. We'll listen, probe, give feed-
back, pray, comfort, care. It doesn't work magic, but it does permit
the continuing flow of grieving if that is what is required.

My husband has also been rediscovering *community* with a group of
his male friends. They meet at the pub on Wednesdays for cheap
chicken wings and beer and talk deep. They work through personal
issues and "marriage stuff" and grieve their own losses of all sorts—

from divorce to unemployment to deteriorating health to the death of dreams. And they laugh.

At our house, we feed people. Like my nana in the 1930s, who would serve dinner to the railway staff from the roundhouse where my grandpa worked, and like my mom in the 1970s, who would provide food for the hippies who traipsed through our home, Russ and I have made it a priority to consistently extend hospitality. We have chosen to make it a habit to regularly prepare dinners for at least ten to fifteen people (ours is a family of five), so that anyone who might be around at suppertime could enjoy a meal with us. It helps to remind everyone that they are never alone—there is always a place you can go; a group of people you can talk to; a person to have tea with, to watch TV with, to laugh with—and we laugh a lot. This restores a bit of our sense of community.

Some members of the group have even taken it upon themselves to create one meal a week and have made a gourmet spread for the whole crowd, which always turns into an evening of celebration with everyone pitching in to produce the feast. In this culture of busyness, typified by meals alone and easy access to fast food, enjoying and making meals together gives everyone a sense of connectedness and belonging. Particularly in the case of young adults (the main crowd that hangs around our place), a communal meal gives them a place to touch down for fraternity, compassion, and friendship as they begin to experience life away from their own families. And there is quite simply something magical about eating together—taking time out during a busy day to hear from one another, to be known, to enjoy living. It fills our souls as much as it fills our bellies.

I will pause here for a little side note. This type of living does not come without some cost to our family—personally, relationally, and financially—and we have, for the most part, accepted this cost, because we feel that the benefits far outweigh the sacrifices. I do acknowledge, though, that there have been times when we have not always gotten the balance of family and extended community quite right. We have lost some of our family traditions, some of our one-on-one time, some of our privacy, some of our *me-time*.

We trust, though, that grace, forgiveness, and our sincere love and concern for our daughters will cover these missteps. And what we have lost has been replaced by more people to share our love with, more people to enrich the lives of our daughters, more people to share in our daily responsibilities (a last-minute pick-up from school, a dog-sitter, another set of hands to help with dinner), more people to do things with, more people to laugh with and process life with. The great by-product in our daughters' lives is that they have become gracious, generous, open-hearted young women who are noted for their love and encouragement of others.

Stability

And although people come and go from the group, *the community continues*. The community endures where individual relationships are impermanent. This, I would suggest, is a great stabilizing force in the transient and ever-changing relational bonds that characterize our current culture. I recently chatted with a young, single woman who lamented, "Man, it just happened again. I just finally found someone that I feel I can fully share my heart with and now she's moving away. Why does this always happen to me?"

What my friend is lamenting is common, especially where there is a trend to marry later; to segregate into generational groupings; to pursue careers and educations away from extended long-term friendships and family. Our society seems wired for isolation.

In the relational community around our home, we have had to become exceedingly pragmatic in terms of care and support. At one point, one young woman in the group, Jane, was in the throes of a struggle with self-hatred, fear, and depression. She was spending more and more time alone at her apartment, not answering calls or emails. When we discovered that it had been many days since any of us had seen or heard from her, we became concerned, and finally went to track her down. Banging incessantly on her door until she answered, two of us were let in by our beautiful friend in all of her disheveled and miserable glory. She didn't know where to start, what to say—she was stuck in the muddle of her sense of worthlessness, of failure, of hopelessness.

As we let her pour out the clutter of her pain and emotional struggle, I suddenly got a hilarious picture in my mind of Jane attempting
to run from the group of us, but we were literally *stapled* to her heels
and she was subsequently dragging us all behind her in the dirt. In
my mind's eye, we were covered in the dust and the debris she was
kicking up behind her in her flight. I sensed that she needed to
know, and so told her, that no matter her need to run, she was stuck
with us until she chose to disconnect from us—in love and support,
we were stapled to her. For this young woman, whose father had
abandoned her family when she was a young teen, fidelity was something she desperately needed to know. She needed the assurance
that we would stick with her no matter what.

Grieving of all sorts needs this sense of constancy—a community
of supporters who are in it for the long haul. Isolation can lead to
despair when the painful flood of grieving begins, but a circle of
companions can step in, even at inconvenient moments, to prevent
a friend from being swept away by hopelessness.

The key is to have a collection of others on whom we can lean and
for whom we can be a support. This gives us hope, and ultimately
resurrects meaning from life.

And for those of us who find ourselves offering or providing support, what do grievers need from us? They need us to listen. To let
them tell their stories. To validate their pain. To weep with them. To
not try to *fix* it. To not judge.

Community is all about the ebb and flow of leaning, and it works
for grieving souls.

8

dulling the pain

They are three siblings, each dealing with the double grief of losing a hard father, prone to belittling them, whose sudden passing after an intense bout with cancer had allowed little time to heal the fragmented father-child relationship and had hindered their grieving. Each sibling had, at a young age, succumbed to the dictate of perfectionism, a direct result of rigid paternal control. Strangely, that pressure to be perfect manifested itself in three very different ways.

The eldest's response typified the perfectionist conditions that had permeated her childhood home. Every aspect of her personal life was immaculate. Every item in her living space had its place, nothing was ever out of order. Everything in her daily existence, from her job to her physical health and her eating habits, was faultless. Any household cleaning was accomplished on a daily, sometimes hourly basis. Vacuuming and dusting were done so frequently that not a single speck of dust, dirt, or lint was permitted to reside on any floor, any piece of furniture, any window sill. Her pursuit of a flawless existence was rigorous and acute.

For the youngest, everything was internalized, and she simply became a driven performer in every area of her life: strong physically, strong emotionally, strong in discipline. Her mantra had come from her father: "Survival of the fittest—the weak won't survive." And she lived by it! She was determined to never be a loser. She rose to the top in her career, in her friendships, in her standing with leaders and bosses. From the outside, she was balanced and successful in all she did. But she had a secret. She would privately obsess over little things—the exact placement of utensils on a table, the position of a chair in a room, the way she would lock the doors at night—until she could put them exactly right.

For the middle child, the only son, the perfectionism was turned on its head and presented itself as a whole collection of failing and hopeless behaviors. Unwittingly, his manner of coping had been to do the very opposite of everything his father had pushed his children to aspire to. It was almost as though his internal response had been, "If I can't do it perfectly, I won't do it at all." Where his father valued athleticism, he became completely physically inactive. Where his father valued a healthy lifestyle, he struggled with obsessive eating and obesity, secretly hiding food in his room in order to gorge in private, away from his father's judgmental badgering. Where his father prized cleanliness and order, his life became a swamp of filth, chaos, and hoarding. Dirty dishes piled up for weeks—months—and were covered with the remnants of food turning furry with mold. Heaps of papers, magazines, books—all littered with the debris of food wrappers, boxes, empty bottles, and yogurt containers—overran the floor space, leaving little room to walk, sit, or even sleep. Whole populations of living creatures had set up home—fruit flies swarmed on the rotting fruit left on counters; whole families of cockroaches had quietly put down roots under the heaps of garbage, establishing a whole cockroach city complete with a full nursery of incubating spawn.

What was the cause of these extreme behaviors? Intuitively, these siblings sensed its root: this was their subconscious way of managing the insurmountable pain of their father's disapproval, criticism, anger, and emotional neglect combined with the suspended grief of his passing. It was each sibling's way of preventing and/or anesthetizing his/her pain.

Not all coping mechanisms are so extreme, but we each have distinctive approaches to reducing the intensity of our agonies. A businessman might lose himself in his work. A mother might find comfort in overeating. A teenager might escape into video games or music or socializing. A student might defer grieving by immersing himself in his studies. But it's all a big cover-up. The truth is, there is no escaping the pain, there is only delay. It will still hurt as much later as it does when it is fresh.

Of the three siblings, only the youngest has been able see progressive changes in her thought patterns and behaviors as she has processed her grief. She has allowed herself to feel her pain, and dances daily. This keeps her connection to her physical self and helps to lift the weight of loss from her body. But further, she was able to talk with her father shortly before his death—and he apologized for his unkindness and his criticizing. She was also able to forgive him. A few years later, she was able to weep over the pain stemming from both his emotional abuse and his early loss. Gradually, this daughter has even addressed her patterns of perfectionism, her need for control, and many of her compulsive behaviors have begun to disappear.

Pain relief

If there is one common aim among those experiencing chronic grief and loss, it is the longing to dull the pain. And if you can't remove the source of the pain, you can at least remove the sensation of it. Journalist Norman Cousins noted that, "For years we have had it drummed into us ... that any hint of pain is to be banished, as though it were the ultimate evil."[25] We have become a generation of expert anesthetizers, avoiding pain at all costs.

Social scientist Brene Brown addresses the issue further. In response to the question of "why we numb," she suggests that often it is to "make everything that is uncertain, certain." And, she adds, it is how we "discharge pain and discomfort."[26]

I have a radical suggestion: Perhaps feeling pain is a good thing. It is what stops us from continuing to do something that will inevitably cause greater damage. It is essential for survival. Dr. Paul Brand, a renowned surgeon who worked for many decades with people with leprosy, had some profound thoughts about pain. Leprosy damages nerve cells, leading to a loss of sensitivity and of the ability to feel pain in the areas affected. Dr. Brand discovered that people with leprosy, and who had lost the ability to feel physical pain, lacked the physical sensitivity to know when to stop applying pressure (twisting a door handle, kicking a tree, pulling a rope) with their fingers, hands, toes. Where a person with healthy sensitivities will stop (pushing, pulling, striking) when he feels pain, a person with leprosy will continue until he has done noticeable damage to his body (ripping the skin, breaking bones, burning flesh).

Dr. Brand declared, "If there is one gift I could give my leprosy patients, it would be the gift of pain." He believed that pain should be embraced for what it is: "our most significant trauma alert system."[27] It is our body's way of focusing our attention on something that we would rather ignore. Dr. Brand believed that pain is something that adds to your life rather than takes away from it, and suggested that sometimes managing pain is more important, ultimately more helpful, than eliminating it.

Regarding the emotional pain of grief, in order to really deal with this sort of pain, it seems best to choose to be vulnerable. Those who choose to simply cope must numb their vulnerability. Brene Brown observed that "You can't selectively numb emotion. When we numb grief and pain ... we also numb joy, gratitude and happiness."[28]

Numbing is not just the anesthetizing of our pain, it is the avoidance of vulnerability. I have seen the results of this in those I have mentored. A flatness develops in their personalities because their choice to resist vulnerability virtually locks down the dynamic aspects of their characters. They don't laugh much; they don't feel compassion easily; they don't respond with excitement to celebrations; they don't, in general, enjoy life much.

How do people numb? I've made a note of a few of the strategies people commonly use to inoculate themselves: *positive thinking, perfection*, and *addictions*.

Positive thinking

Positive thinking may seem a *reasonable* approach to coping in the light of this being a book in pursuit of hope after grief. Surely, you might reason, looking at a situation positively can help to ease the pain of loss. If you can bear with me on this, I hope that you will see why I see it as a rather less healthy approach. I have a friend who is constantly injuring herself. In her teens, her youthful zeal and recklessness resulted in multiple accidents, injuries, myriad close calls. She miraculously survived every incident, but she was always getting hurt.

As an adult she experienced dramatic back pain—pain so excruciating that it would even cause her to throw up. On one occasion, she mentioned to me that she had been experiencing an unusually high level of pain. I asked her, "Isn't there something that your doctor can give you for the pain?" "Oh yes," she replied, "I have some painkillers, but I'm not taking them." "Why in the world wouldn't you?" I declared. "You know me," was her response, "if I can't feel the pain, I'll do something stupid!"

I get a sense that positive thinking can be like a pain-masking drug—it does not make the source of the pain (or the injury or the infection) go away; it simply pauses the sensation for a time.

Immediately following the death of my mother, there was no shortage of positive thinkers storming the bastion of my grief. "Aren't you grateful that she didn't suffer for long?" "Isn't it a relief that you know she has gone to Heaven?" "She was a good mom. You are blessed to have had her for as long as you did!" There was nothing particularly wrong with any of these well-meaning comments, but it was at a time, just days after my mom's passing, that I could only feel pain. It hurt that my mom was no longer with me; that she had died so quickly; that there were so many things I still wanted to say to her, still wanted to do with her; that I couldn't do anything to make her better; that she was gone forever. It was a pain I needed, wanted, to feel.

To quote Dr. Maté:

> As soon as we qualify the *thinking* with the adjective *positive*, we exclude those parts of reality that strike us as *negative* ... "positive thinking" is based on an unconscious belief that we are not strong enough to handle reality ... The power of negative thinking requires the strength to accept that we are not as strong as we would like to believe.[29]

I agree with Dr. Maté, and suggest that there are times when our *positive thinking* is a counterproductive strategy when grieving. It single-handedly removes my permission to acknowledge the awful things that sometimes go through my mind and affect my emotions as I am grieving. "I hate that he has done this!" "I am so angry at what has happened!" "I just want to die!" Smoothing these dark sentiments over with *positivity* simply locks them in chains and throws them into the dungeon of our psyche. They are inclined to fret and fume and rise up as a rebellious force against our soul's security, inflicting physical, emotional, and psychological ruin on our beings.

Certainly, there might come a time in the grieving process when a person may need to encourage herself to leave a place of self-pity, but that will only come after adequate attention has been paid to the scope of the loss and the pain.

Perfection

If there is one thing a person feels desperate to do after a loss, it is to try to *make sure* that it never happens again. For example, the emotionally abused child may work to *become the perfect child* so that the parent won't get angry with him again. A mother who has lost a baby and discovers she is pregnant again may strive to make everything in her life ideal to ensure that nothing will interfere with the survival of the new baby. An entrepreneur who has gone bankrupt may be cautious and overly calculating about his next project.

Thinking back to my dad's family, in their need to control how they were perceived by their fellow Canadians, their loyalty thermometer was continuously scrutinized in all sorts of hidden ways. My aunts and uncles often made a habit of ensuring that all the siblings and grandchildren did everything *just so* so as to not offend anyone around them. Apologies, appeasements, *proper behavior* were constantly urged, checked, and double-checked, even as the grandchildren approached middle age.

Unfortunately, each of these strategies will often result in added stress, missteps, fear, people-pleasing, or anxiety. The pursuit of perfection will not necessarily prevent subsequent loss or even remove the sting of current pain. The ungrieved heartache will continue as a lingering sorrow, hidden beneath the calm exterior of perfection until it is properly addressed, like the heat of an infection festering under the surface of unblemished skin.

The experience of pain is something Kristina, a young woman of just 19, had been avoiding. Kristina is the eldest daughter in a family of four children. Her parents separated and then divorced when she was still in elementary school. As the firstborn, she took it upon herself to bring peace to the household in as many ways as possible. She was *the perfect child*. If her father required something of her, she was always readily available, even though on many occasions he would make promises to do something for her or with her and then cancel. When her mother returned from work, exhausted and easily irritated, Kristina made sure that the house was in order and that her siblings were doing their part to alleviate their mother's workload. When her father was out of work, she stressed herself out by taking on his fears and concerns. When her siblings were ill or under emotional stress, she would fret about their well-being.

In short, on many levels, Kristina had become the rescuer of the family—and she was paying for it. Not only was all this stress taking its toll on her emotions (increasing fear and anger), her character (she had developed a *flatness* of emotional response), and her physical health (she had an ulcer by the age of 15), but it was also masking her actual root issue, which was that she had never grieved the loss of her father in the household or her parents' marriage. Emotionally, her sensitivity to the pain of her loss had numbed itself. She had been unable to feel anything—about the situation, about her own emotions, about joy, about pain. Presumably, the emotional shutdown began way back when she was a child and her father had left.

When she finally began to allow herself to feel the pain, it was as though something was reviving itself in her, but it was not a gentle process. She was afraid of exposing her family; she was afraid to show weakness; she was afraid that her facade of perfection would be taken away; she was afraid to acknowledge how much her father had let them all down.

As she allowed the pain to surface, the sobbing began. This dancer, who had had no voice in her family, and who was finding herself feeling new emotions for which she had no words, used dance to speak the words she could not. She found that there was a grating in her being that could only be expressed with the grinding of her tap shoes on the floor—circling and sliding her tap-shod feet pendulum-like along the floor and generating a scraping, swooshing, abrasive sound over and over. It was the sound of what was going on in her internally—no utterance, only a deep *sense* of distress and turmoil that seemed to have no outlet. She added it to the dance piece she was creating. She was distressed to realize that her father had never been emotionally available to her and her siblings; to realize that in many ways he had actually taken advantage of her. She ached as she understood that she had been carrying her mother's pain. Her agony poured out as she finally recognized that she was mostly disappointed with God. As a child, she had prayed with a group of friends at her Christian school that God would stop her parents from divorcing, but they still had. She was left with a vexing belief that God had let her down.

These imperfect but important and very real sentiments clearly clashed with her perfectionistic habits. She began to recognize that her quest for perfection had done nothing to prevent pain, had not produced an increased affirmation of her worth, and had not been successful in creating an environment of peace. Ultimately, she no longer needed the facade of perfection. Bit by bit, like a sprout emerging from the ground, her real self, a fullness of emotion and character, began to poke through. Her own needs started to find their place and her sense of value began to emerge.

Addictions

The third coping mechanism, and undoubtedly one of the most prevalent pain-deadening instruments chosen by scores of people worldwide, is the abuse and misuse of addictive substances, activities, or behaviors. Their scope is endless: from food to drugs; from overwork to alcohol; from extreme sports to sex. Some of these pain alleviators are so socially acceptable that they are not frequently acknowledged as potentially problematic. Others cause such a dependency, and console such a depth of pain, that their hold is exceedingly difficult to break. And yet, the habit is not so much the target problem but rather the pain and the need to process the tormenting grief.

Edgar Allan Poe described the hold that addictive substances had on him:

> I have absolutely no pleasure in the stimulants in which I sometimes so madly indulge. It has not been in the pursuit of pleasure that I have periled life and reputation and reason. It has been in the desperate attempt to escape from the torturing memories, from a sense of insupportable loneliness and a dread of some strange impending doom.[30]

The Aboriginal people of Canada have been at the center of some of Canada's more damaging histories of pain, loss, and grief. My experience of them is that they are a noble people lost in hopelessness, fear, rejection, and despair. Addictions, arising from the need for solace and as a means to escape pain, are often the consequence of trying to anesthetize their agony, with alcohol and drug dependencies being the most common escape measures. Thankfully, over the last few years, Canada has begun to look at the plight of the indigenous population and is initiating a process of addressing the injustices that have been done to them.[31] For the first time in more than a century and a half, Canada's First Peoples have started to speak about the horrific experiences of their past and have begun to allow the surge of sorrow, giving birth to restoration.

In the summer of 2010, I sat in a crowded arena in Ottawa for the *Forgiven Summit*, a *reconciliation initiative* spearheaded by a group of First Nations leaders. Two years previously, Prime Minister Stephen Harper had extended an apology to the First Peoples for the wrongs and abuses that had been done to many of them at the hands of staff in government-run residential schools (1840s–1996). The Forgiven Summit was an opportunity for these Native people to extend forgiveness. I sat riveted, stunned by the painstaking detail and weighty sentiment of the recollections that the aging generation of Aboriginal men and women began to share from the microphone. At this national event, none of us were quite prepared for the heartbreaking stories that we were about to hear.

Some were as young as 5 years old when they were taken from their homes, at times forcibly, to comply with the national law that made it compulsory for all Aboriginal children under the age of 16 to attend residential schools in order to *civilize and assimilate them*.[32] Stripped of their identity, their culture, their language, their communities, and their families, many of these children had endured physical, psychological, and even sexual abuse by school staff, and sometimes even by older students. Illness (resulting in a mortality rate of 30%–60%), malnutrition, squalid living conditions, and, for some, nothing more than a nominal education were all that many of them received in exchange for the separation from their families. Most emerged shell-shocked and broken, and, as one woman put it, "We became adults who didn't even know how to parent our own children." Subsequently, the cycle of hopelessness, desperation, addiction, and suicide begun by earlier generations has carried on among First Nations youth—suicide rates being four times greater than the national average (for the Inuit the rate is even higher, being eleven times greater than the national average).

And yet, amazingly, throughout the Forgiven Summit was a constant, unexpected glimmer of hope. Many of the testimonials also included the accounts of those who had weathered their afflictions and addictions and had managed to find restoration through forgiving those who had abused them. Many also found peace. For some, by recovering their honor for their elders and ancestors; for others, through a faith in God; and still others, by restoring key facets of their neglected First Nations culture. These formerly tormented individuals had managed to confront their pain head-on, had shed its weight, and had cultivated a whole new, productive life. The noble gathering of men and women who stood before us on that day was a miracle on a magnificent scale. They had become gracious, humble, compassionate, beautiful, and truly joyful people.

Devastation looked set to turn to resolution. Government representatives were in attendance, repeating publicly once again the apology that had been first declared by the prime minister two years earlier. Words of forgiveness were extended by First Nations elders and chiefs, accompanied by a bounty of gifts—blankets, traditional clothing, jewelry—as a visible demonstration of this forgiveness.

For many, though, the journey to freedom is still not over, as hopelessness continues to plague families and Native reserves suffer high rates of suicide and addiction. But in the words of songwriter Bruce Cockburn, we've "got to kick at the darkness 'til it bleeds daylight."[33]

The restoration of the First Nations Aboriginal culture has been a powerful healing force to liberate many individuals from their dependency on addictive substances. The very thing that had been deemed *uncivilized*[34] by the founding government of Canada has become the beauty and potency of a people. The reclaiming of cultural dances, rituals, and artistic expressions, the rebuilding of family, and the restoration of Aboriginal community leadership have proved invaluable in resurrecting the worth of the Native People.

Expressions of the revived Native culture were overflowing at the Forgiven Summit. Along with the magnificent regalia, Native drums, songs, and chants, the gift-giving rituals, and declarations of honor was the most central of their Native expressions: dance. It was their most ready response to these historic proceedings.

Throughout the conference, dance seemed to be a natural demonstration of their restoration. A grand processional dance opened the whole event—young women and girls stomping and twirling in brightly colored fringed dresses and feather headbands; chiefs and important elders in full headdresses shuffling to the rhythm of the drum; and warriors whirling and stamping, standing guard at the rear.

In addition, a visiting group of Samoans stepped onto the stage to perform a haka, which unleashed power in a whole other dimension. They called for the return of the First Nations warriors—those young Native Canadian men—who had been hiding out in their pain. Many of them came forward. Some stood and wept, recognizing that their sorrow over their loss of courage and honor had left them incapacitated. The haka seemed to fill them with hope. By the end of the conference, everyone was on their feet. The whole audience was dancing en masse across the stage—shuffling, hopping, twirling to the distinctive Native rhythm on the drums and guitars. Movement let loose by the joy of freedom to be the people they were created to be.

What had been essential, and critical, for any of this delicate mending of relationships? Undoubtedly, a safe and trustworthy environment where honor, humility, and kindness were foundational. So what happens when the circumstances are not so safe? What transpires when protective responses are in play?

9

defending, burden-bearing
and present danger

When I was growing up, I knew that my father lived constantly with silent fears and anxieties. Whenever we approached the border between Canada and the USA as we headed to our summer vacation spot, Dad would become agitated and fearful. I never knew why. It was not until many years later that he finally confessed. "As a teenager, due to the governmental restrictions on Canadians of Japanese descent, we were never allowed to cross the border. I have since developed a secret fear that I will be *discovered*, arrested, and sent back."

For most of my life, I was barely aware of the story of my father's family and their oppression during and following World War II. The injustice of this violation of rights and liberties was never spoken of while I was growing up. There seemed to be a silent pact between the members of his family to not lay blame. Did they perhaps fear being accused of ill will toward Canada?

Like a fugitive fleeing her captors and striving to keep her child quiet during their flight, any complaints or cries of injustice from my father's family members were quickly silenced. Town leaders and government authorities were staunchly defended by his parents and silently obeyed by all, while a hidden sea of agitations and fears foamed in the hearts of the children. Regardless, prejudice against Dad's family increased day by day. The girls, my father's sisters, were incessantly bullied on their two-mile walk to school each day. My father's Japanese looks—the prominent teeth and slanty eyes, the stuff of caricatured stereotypes prevalent in wartime newspapers and comic strips—were the object of ridicule. Their exclusion from crowds of friends and neighborhood relationships caused my father and his siblings to live with a persistent sense of alienation.

The shame of simply being Japanese became a thing of apology and may have even provided grounds for the family's defense of the nation's racial bigotry. My father admits to having a disdain for his Japanese heritage, vowing to never speak the Japanese language that was regularly spoken in his home. He even tried in vain to make his eyes, his distinctively Japanese-looking eyes, *not slanty*. And against this backdrop, my father's family was simply never able to address, or discuss with anyone, the impact, the pain of how they were treated.

How is it that we can become so skilled at defending those circumstances, those individuals who have hit us with the hardest blows? How is it that our well-developed sense of justice can evaporate when we have become the target of injustice? I see it as a device to protect those we love, even if they have wronged us in some way. I sense it arises when we have expected a life of relative peace and contentment—it becomes a barricade, a lovely picket fence that closes off a painful truth. I understand as well that it can even be a desperate effort to retain some sense of normalcy in the midst of dysfunction and ongoing distress. Inevitably, though, these types of protective responses inhibit our grieving.

Defending

With respect to Dad's family, I recognize that they felt the need to *defend* the actions of their government and to protect what little reputation they might be able to salvage from their experience. There seemed to be a perception among them that they were "not worthy of protection." What had inadvertently evolved was a general belief that everyone *outside* the family was right—others and their needs were to be valued as more important than the needs and concerns of the family. If something had gone wrong in a relationship, it was the family member who was at fault; if there was a complaint about unfair treatment, the family member would be reprimanded for *making waves*.

A similar thread winds through the lives of many who have experienced loss, abuse, injustice. A man who is verbally, emotionally abused by his supervisor might excuse the behavior: "He's under a lot of stress." "I said something that *triggered* his frustration. I should have known better." Why does the man defend his boss? Perhaps fear, perhaps perfectionism as connected to his own concerns about failure. He might even be echoing the supervisor's own justifications for his actions—his own fears of failure may cause him to blame-shift to his co-workers.

Or a person may begin *placating* as a coping mechanism to protect against the malicious behavior of another. In order to dodge an anticipated response of anger from her abusive husband, a wife might make a special meal, just so he feels happier; or she might avoid talking about anything that would touch off his anger; or she might even try to control what others say and do around him in order to create the *perfect environment* for him. But it rarely works—placating only *validates and enables* the disagreeable behavior. Addressing the behavior head-on is not only critical for the abuser to begin to change this damaging pattern, it is also the only way that his wife can begin to heal from the abuse.

Very often, fears of dishonoring someone, of being disloyal, or of exposing someone can lead to hurtful behavior being sidestepped. A controlling person can even persuade another that any disclosure of *the truth* is a betrayal of the relationship. Ultimately, these all suppress the acknowledgment of the pain inflicted. And that hinders grieving.

Burden-bearing

To add another facet to this scenario, if a person is of the more accommodating personality type, another inhibitor can often be added to grieving: *burden-bearing*.

Throughout her formative years, Dana had endured a painful relationship with her mother. She couldn't recall ever having pleased her mom—from what she wore to what she did. If she was upstairs when her mother burned a cake in the kitchen, her mother would yell for Dana to come down and then proceed to blame her for the ruined cake because she wasn't helping. If she was in the kitchen helping her mother and a cake burned, her mother would vent her frustration at Dana. This became a consistent pattern from the time she was small until she was in her twenties. Dana actually had no memories of words of kindness, affirmation, or affection—her mother seemed constantly consumed with anger.

In her late teens, she had uncovered a secret bargain her mother and father had made in her early years. Her parents had negotiated with one another that they would each take responsibility for one of their two children—her mother would care for her older sister and her father would care for Dana. This did not prove to be a healthy arrangement, especially as they were all living together in one house. Dana's sister had been a difficult child, and her mother consequently felt frustrated in her parenting—she felt like a failure. That frustration was curiously redirected toward Dana, the *better behaved* child whom Dad was overseeing, because she served to reinforce Mom's sense of failure as a parent. What this ultimately produced in Dana was a profound sense that her mother did not care about her and/ or that she was simply an annoyance to her mother.

Dana grew up with a deep and gnawing hunger for the approval of her mother. She worked hard to please her, giving and serving beyond all reasonable expectation, but never attaining her goal. No matter how hard she tried, no matter what she did, her mother could never be satisfied and would never praise her. By the time she was in her teens, Dana decided to give up on the idea of pleasing her mother and began instead to express a disdain for her mother through her words and her actions. If her mother didn't care about her, she wouldn't care about her mother.

And so it continued through to her early adulthood—a nagging disconnect between mother and daughter. It was during an exceedingly volatile argument with her mother that Dana finally let loose with her real emotions. "Why can't you love me?" she blurted. Silence hung between them for a moment, but then her mother countered with "I do love you!!" At that moment something shifted—years of animosity seemed suddenly breached. And then, wonder of all wonders, they even embraced.

Though Dana's mother still struggled to speak encouraging words to her, things continued to shift. On the day of her wedding, Dana finally heard the words "You are beautiful" from her mother. She was stunned. She suddenly began to build a happy relationship with her mother. It was a time of incredible breakthrough in their kindness to one another, and Dana became a passionate champion of her mother. The sudden gift of her mother's affections was food to a starving child; years of harsh behavior were being washed away. Her mother became her hero.

But what of the wounds to the child from all those years of unjust treatment? Were they truly washed away? With her mother's approval secured, Dana didn't want anything to jeopardize this precious new relationship. She unknowingly chose to whitewash over the wrongs of the past, and had no idea that the years of such rejection had shaped not only her opinion of herself, but also the way she approached relationships. If anyone attempted to point out the need for Dana to grieve the pain that had been inflicted on her throughout her youth by her mother's cruelty, Dana would staunchly deny that it had had an impact, affirming that her mom had been the best mother a child could ever have.

She would dismiss the unpleasant interactions between her and her mother, expressing sympathy for the difficult position her mother had been in because she was raising a difficult child. She even insisted that the things of the past were washed away and didn't affect her anymore, and chose instead to carry the weight of her mother's transgressions upon herself, covering the wounds and excusing the wrongs. But the pain was there, and it took a wise counselor to begin to unpack the heartache of rejection, the agony of verbal abuse, and the distress of not knowing a mother's love. Gradually, she began to acknowledge the sense of loss and the feelings of worthlessness, to grieve the truth of how it had affected her on many fronts throughout her life. Her marriage had become the place where her past had manifested in the most destructive way. She had chosen a man who didn't love her very well—he too would never show her affection or tell her that she was beautiful. She spent much of her marriage trying to please and appease, always concluding that she was never enough for him, or in fact for anyone. Eventually, she began to connect her lifelong struggle with a lack of self-worth to the devastating absence of her mother's approval.

She began the *working out* of her sense of grief and loss through music and dance, but gradually introduced an even more powerful bodily expression/outlet: extreme sports. The physical exertion brings emotional release for all sorts of lingering, pained sentiments—even her coach keeps her connected body, soul, and spirit as she is training so that she moves forward equally in her athletic technique and in life.

A highly compassionate person may struggle to acknowledge, and sometimes to accept, the magnitude of wrongs done to them and to others. Why? For one, a compassionate person is predisposed to see the best in people—they see others' redeeming qualities; they believe in rehabilitation. For another, they often hope for a positive relationship with the abuser, perhaps buoyed by a sense of seeing the oppressor's struggles and *who they really are*. A dominating thought can pervade: "No one understands them like I do. I am the only one *on their side*." This sort of defense is rooted in burden-bearing. Out of our love and care for others, we often cover for them, excuse them, lament with them over the injustices they have suffered and are suffering.

To be able to have such a depth of compassion for others is a great gift. It is mercy in its elementary form. But it can create a lopsided relationship: one person taking everything and one giving everything. It leaves one person carrying the hefty weight of another's damaging behavior and destructive interactions while disregarding their own well-being. Renowned author, inner-healing expert, and founder of Elijah House John Sandford has said that those who are burden-bearers carry a sense of the ideal of how things were meant to be and long to see things manifest within the parameters of that ideal.

According to Sandford, if a person does not find an adequate way to release the burdens, there is a tendency to become *depressed* or *critical* (of others). He recommends prayer as the ideal way to manage these burdens; he believes that to lay them out before a greater authority places them in the hands of one who truly has the ability to carry the burden of another's failings. The more a person can lift these burdens (people) off their shoulders—the emotional concern, the relational weight—the greater peace can be felt, the greater relief can be gained, the greater attention can be focused on personal need. I would add to that suggestion a visualization: placing the offending person in a basket and pushing them far away, enabling the sufferer to distance themselves from that person and the associated pain.[35]

My burden-bearing is of the critical sort. My constant complaint is, "If he could just get his act together, I wouldn't have to be so miserable!" "If she could just stop being so unkind, I wouldn't be so stressed out!" This too hinders grieving because I end up caught up in a person's plight until they manage to see what they are inflicting on others or on themselves. Anxiety, anger, and bitterness can plague my peace until I lift those individuals off my shoulders through prayer.

Burden-bearers mourn because they ache for kindness, for peace, for loving relationships, for honor, for care. These noble ideals arise in the face of injustices of all sorts: children were not meant to be abused by their parents; spouses were not meant to be cheated on; citizens were not meant to be oppressed by their governments; the needy were not meant to be kept in poverty by uncaring communities; teenagers were not meant to be preyed on or cyber-bullied by malicious strangers. Finding a means to release this grief is essential for those who carry these burdens.

This might sound a little strange, but I sometimes express my prayers through symbolic movement. When I am concerned about the injustice of those who are being oppressed by abusive others, I dance out the breaking of chains and the severing of unhealthy relationships. When I see a person unaware of their ill-treatment of those closest to them, I demonstrate in movement an opening of the eyes, of the mind to understanding. I'm not sure what, if anything, it does to change the situation, but it for sure helps me to let go of the weight of my wordless concern, because that too can get trapped in my body (the fear, the anger) and needs to be physically released.

Present danger

One further motivation can produce a protective response, and this one arises when the safety of an individual is still in jeopardy. If a threat to health remains after a severe illness has been weathered; if the aftermath of a natural disaster has left homes, food sources, and daily needs precarious; if an abuser is still in the household where the victim lives—these present dangers make it impossible for grief to be addressed.

Returning to our experience with the Rwandan widows, for seven years these women had had to remain in their state of unresolved grief. One of the main reasons was the prevailing fear that the killers were still around or even that their neighbors might still rise up against them. An overall reticence had rendered the entire population mute and no one dared speak about their devastating experiences. Many of the people we spoke with chose to lie about their family's relationships and origins (aligning themselves with one or the other of the two warring tribes) in order to preserve their safety.

Most of the 150 women who gathered on the lawn of the convent that second day of our visit had not dared go near the grounds of the facility since the week, seven years earlier, when the Mother Superior and her assistant had corralled their loved ones in the outbuildings of the convent grounds. Although it had been the militia who had proceeded to pour the gas over the buildings and burn those several thousand people alive, it had been the Mother Superior who had called the militia. She had handed them the cans of gas and had given them permission to begin to burn the buildings. The survivors, these 150 women who met with us, were terrified that someone might do the same to them these many years later.

Providentially, during the time that we were at the convent, the Mother Superior and her assistant had removed themselves to Belgium. With the present danger (the two offending nuns) eliminated, it was the right time for this collection of bereaved women to be able to return to the place of their loss and begin to face the immense grief that had never been addressed. The presence of women from Canada seemed to provide safety, a sense that their well-being would be protected; a sense that they had the freedom to begin to allow the pain to pour out its agony.

(A further benediction was added the very week of our return to Canada. There, in the headlines of our Canadian newspapers, were photos of those two nuns, the Mother Superior and her assistant, being hauled away by the Belgian police after being arrested, tried, and convicted for the murder of the thousands of Rwandans who had taken sanctuary at their facility. Miraculous!)

There is unquestionably a critical need for the griever to remove the present danger (or remove oneself from it), when the time is right, so that unseen losses can be grieved in a secure environment. But note that the safety of the place/people where the refuge is found is also critical. Judgments, controlling behavior, and breaches of confidentiality can shatter the fragile emotional state of a sufferer who is ready to grieve. Compassion, care, grace, and a listening ear are the mourner's protective walls.

But even with external dangers removed, sometimes grieving still does not flow.

10

angry sediment and bitter waters

She sits in the dimness so that he can barely see her. As his eyes adjust to the darkness, he can suddenly make out the form of a woman; she is still, as though time has ossified her in the dusty seat where she reclines. Her silvery hair, though now disheveled, appears to have once known curl and intentional design—was that a flower behind the ear, now dried and beginning to crumble? She is evidently sheathed in a gown of sorts—the intricacies of the fabric indicated the happiness of lace, but it was yellowed, unhappily dingy.

As he looks about, he sees that the entire room seems to have been peppered with gray dust. Here, a once silver hairbrush and matching hand mirror. There, a collection of dust-laden china ornaments, barely visible photographs, and faded Oriental boxes, each purposefully perched on dejected doilies. In the corner, on an elegantly carved antique parlor table, gritty with layers of settled soot from the smoldering hearth, is a tilting tower of stiff, round slabs—a wedding cake, perhaps? The whole frosty edifice is oddly dotted with pale floral contours that seem to have turned to stone, perhaps marble, a reflection of the woman who sits nearby.

This is how I picture Pip's first meeting with Miss Havisham in Charles Dickens's *Great Expectations*.[36] At the risk of doing a disservice to his more eloquent description, I hoped that this briefer image would give you the impression that comes to my mind when I think of this forlorn character in Dickens's portrayal of jilted love. If you have not read the story, Miss Havisham, we eventually discover, was a young bride left at the altar on the day of her wedding. She lives perpetually suspended in time, stuck in the very day that her grief was inflicted upon her—in the very clothing, in the very room, with everything as it was; even the clock is stopped at the very time that her hopes for her life were stolen from her.

In her broken and bitter heart is a vendetta against men. She adopts a young girl, Estella, whom she raises to be poised, heartless, and cruel, just so that Miss Havisham can watch her break young men's hearts.

It is sad to say that many of us live with our grief in the very same way, especially if we sense that we have been wronged in any way. We endlessly revisit our memories and replay the event. Anger is sustained, never attended to. Bitterness begins to grow like some untamed weed and our efforts begin to get focused on controlling the world around us so that no one and nothing can hurt us again. The dust begins to settle on this miserable state of being, and before we know it, an eternity has passed and our emotional clocks have stopped. How do we begin to release ourselves from this sad predicament?

It is with this in mind that I return to the stages of grieving and take a look at what might be impeding progression beyond this state. To begin with, anger and blame are powerful, unwieldy, unattractive emotions. In our well-behaved culture, they don't seem to belong, and so we are inclined to *wisely* suppress them. But there is actually no *wisdom* in that. Those emotions brew, boil, and froth in a thousand other ways. There is actually no suppressing them. What is wise is to choose where and to whom these easily misunderstood and easily misused emotions are vented—and to keep them from putting down roots.

Don't "should" on me

I am endlessly challenged on this front. Allowing these messy emotions to come out is a complicated matter. My obstacle? I have an annoying habit in the editing of my thoughts of listening to what I call my *Church lady*. She chides me: "That's not nice to say, you *should* really say_____." "It's okay, it's not worth making an issue of it. You *should* keep the waters calm." "If you really were loving, you wouldn't think that way. You *should* respond with more understanding." That Church lady *should's* on me all the time. She brings condemnation, shame, and fear, and ultimately forces all the intensity of my emotion underground where it bubbles unseen, a hot lava of tumult ready to spew through a weaker outlet like my health or my relationships.

Subsequently, writing has become my best girlfriend—she listens and she doesn't tell me what to do. Writing is where I am able to spill out all the messiness of the blame—the hateful thoughts, the ugly fuming of my reactions—without hurting anyone. It is here that I am able to see all that is going on in my heart—without the Church lady interfering with my thoughts and emotions—and can begin to process the chaos. Sometimes it becomes a prayer of pleading as I lay it out before a greater authority—one who can *take it*; one who sees the injustice that I have suffered; one who can even vindicate me if necessary.

Sometimes, a trusted friend or counselor can take me a little further into those emotions and can become another avenue through which honest expression can pour—but it needs to be someone who is willing to allow me to clean out my junk drawer, as it were. My junk drawer is where I stuff all those extreme emotions that I can't make sense of. Before I know it, it's crammed full of a frustrating assortment of passionate debris that is frightening to begin to sort through. The best course of action is to have a friend who can help to empty out that emotional junk drawer. A friend who won't mind the mess as it spills to the floor. A friend who can help to sort, piece by piece, each pain, each anger, each sorrow, each blame, and put it back in a more manageable state in the drawer of emotions.

Still, how do we deal with all that anger? Anger in its fullness is such an ugly stepsister of an emotion. I don't know about you, but I have little desire to be in the same room with her while she fusses and stomps unreasonably, inflicting her cruel laments on bystanders. I would think that to lock her away and hide the key would seem the most sensible course of action, would it not? But what she actually needs is to be given a voice so that her fury can subside.

One of the most important tasks for a friend or counselor is to give me *permission* to feel whatever I'm feeling. There is no right or wrong when it comes to emotion. Emotions just *are*. How we deal with them becomes either healing to us or impedes us for a lifetime.

Dancing out volatile emotions like anger can be invaluable, and ultimately less damaging than saying angry words or punching someone. Lydia, whose burden of abuse and isolation has left a heavy weight of fury in her, dances with flags circling the slicing the air with vehement force—her angst manifest in powerful flashes of vigorous color and fierce beauty. Ultimately it dissolves her hostility and dissipates her turbulent emotions, giving room for her sadness to be sufficiently expressed.

What happens when our anger gets locked away and is not expressed? It strangely becomes more and more powerful. And make note, in a time when we feel most powerless, anger makes us feel powerful. It is why it ultimately becomes one of the most difficult emotions to let go of. Power over this situation, over that person, over having to feel the pain of loss again. But this will never offer freedom or peace.

Anger can trap you. I once heard the story of a family who experienced the sudden loss of their daughter in a car accident. It was nighttime, and an unexpected and violent rainstorm had pelted the dark mountain road as a group of friends set out on a camping trip, including the daughter and her husband. Their little Honda had hydroplaned and then spun out on a barren stretch of road, the car flipping and landing in a ditch, leaving the wife unconscious. It was in the days before cell phones and so the husband ordered all his companions to stay with his wife and the car while he walked to find help. The man made it to the nearest town and returned to the accident scene with a rescue crew, but it was too late to save his wife.

The woman's family, in their grief, had swiftly blamed the man for his negligence: had he not left the car, their daughter, his wife, might still be alive today. That blame turned to anger, and they ceased talking to the man; that anger turned to bitterness, and they scorned him, especially when he married again a few years later. The rift between the man's family and his former wife's family remained for decades, even though they lived in the same community and shared the same groups of friends. Hatred, animosity, and coldness persisted for a lifetime, tainting the relationships of children, grandchildren, and friends of these two families.

This is the angry phase of grief left for far too long. It is anger left to fester. Had there perhaps been appropriate processing of grief for all concerned, there may have been a more productive reaction to these painful sentiments. A lifetime is too long to remain captive in the angry grip of loss, and it can not only wreak havoc on a person and their relationships, but also begin to spread.

Bitter root judgments

Anger left in hiding for too long becomes bitterness. Bitterness loves to establish itself in our beings like an annoying dandelion tap root. It begins to infect our assessment of daily realities: people seem crueler, situations seem more unjust, everything seems more irritating. Additionally, the person toward whom this bitterness has developed can become the target of our further judgment, a *bitter root judgment*. A single act of injustice can become a whole litany of offending actions as judged through the filter of bitterness. Every comment starts to be seen as motivated by some malicious intent or deep-seated character failing.

Without a doubt, I have inflicted bitter root judgments on others. I have griped and criticized, lamented and scorned the behaviors of numerous individuals, all to my own detriment. I am sad to admit this, especially as I know firsthand how judgment affects its target.

A few years ago, a group of my friends were severely offended by something I had said. They accurately detected that an emotionally charged comment had actually stemmed from a deep-seated jealousy. Unfortunately, a bitter root took hold, and over the next few years everything I said was suddenly interpreted as coming from my criticism of them or from a fault in my temperament.

Although I had apologized profusely for my unkind comment, whenever I was around them I could detect a thinly veiled contempt for my very presence. Everything I did, everything I said was under question. The turmoil of these interactions left me constantly shrinking and repeatedly cut off from their friendship. I felt I had been virtually locked in prison without a fair trial. It would be several years before that scenario changed. When they finally recognized and acknowledged their bitterness and apologized, I was released from prison. They confessed that *they* had begun to wrongly judge my behavior simply because they had been hurt by that original, admittedly offensive remark.

Bitter root judgments can begin to affect new circumstances (and be directed toward new individuals) that have similar characteristics to the original offense. Now the bitterness starts to impact all sorts of unrelated relationships and begins to surface in unpredictable places.

A number of years ago, I was on a mission with a group of people from all over the world. The group had spent three months in training and then embarked on an international mission to Asia. I had come to know a few members of the team quite well before the trip, but I had had very little interaction with the rest of the team before then. It was therefore surprising that one woman, with whom I had only ever had a couple of actual conversations, was suddenly having enormous issues with me. It became so concerning that she finally booked us into an appointment with the team counselor.

A little confused, I sat in the room with this woman, the counselor, and our husbands to begin a mediation session. The counselor asked me to begin. "What problems, Sandy, do you seem to be having with Melissa?" I quickly scanned my thoughts for some remnant of evil intent, and could only come up with, "I think maybe I haven't been supportive enough of some of the things she has been doing ...?" and then apologized immediately: "Sorry for that."

The counselor then asked the woman, "And what problems do you have with Sandy?" I was paralyzed, stunned, as she began an hour-long rant about all the things that she had against me: a look I had given her; an *underlying meaning* she had deduced from a response to a question she had asked; *hidden implications* in a dozen of my observed behaviors. I was shaking with shock, internally pleading, "But I don't even have enough of a relationship with this woman for her to have so many problems with me!"

Fortunately, my exoneration came in a single statement at the end of her tirade: "She's *just like* ..." and she suddenly spoke the name of a woman (her name, coincidentally, incredibly, was the same as mine) from her hometown against whom she had nurtured a grievance for many years. Was it possible that she had transferred her problems with this woman to me? I pulled the counselor aside after the session and appealed to her: "I don't think these problems are about me, I think she has shifted all of her resentment regarding this other woman to me!" The counselor agreed—there was a bitter root judgment that had been relocated from the relationship at home to this new situation.

We met again after a few days, and I had high hopes that this misplaced judgment might be illuminated by the counselor. However, she didn't mention it as our mediation session began. We sat, just the two of us, with the counselor, and this time she encouraged us to express positive things about one another. I started. I mentioned how I enjoyed Melissa's singing and guitar playing; how I thought she was a strong and visionary leader; how I appreciated her enthusiasm and her sensitivity; how I thought she was a great mom and a fantastic support for her husband. The counselor then asked Melissa, "What good things do you have to say about Sandy?" There was a brief bit of silence as she thought, but then she began "Um-m ... uh-h-h ... oh-h ... uh-h-h ..." I was mortified as she carried on in the same manner for the next several minutes, um-m-ing and uh-h-ing to the deafening silence of the counselor. I looked pleadingly at our mediator in a panicked *please-stop-this-or-I-am-going-to-die* stare, but she did nothing, spoke not a word. It was an agonizing 15 minutes before Melissa finally squeezed out a solitary, "Uh-h she's a pretty good mother ..." I left the session crushed.

Our bitterness spreads. A single offense, festering in my being, can become a mass of offenses that multiply into new situations and affect new people. But a single solution can uproot this infection before it spreads: *forgiveness*. Unforgiveness is the soil in which a bitter root thrives. Forgiveness, however, gets to the very foundation of our bitterness and releases us from its hold.

I know a man who was excluded from his parents' will. His father, who was from the *Old Country*, clung to the belief that the inheritance of properties and homes was the right of eldest sons only, and so although he was given a portion of his parents' liquid assets, he received none of the beautiful buildings and properties that his wealthy father had accumulated in his lifetime. He was angry, and perhaps justifiably so, but instead of weeping over the injustice, he chose to focus his anger on his brother, who had willingly accepted the inheritance and left him with *nothing*. For some fifty years he nurtured a root of bitterness against his brother. Family gatherings were delicate matters, as he could never be invited to any events where his brother might be in attendance and vice versa.

His bitterness spilled over into other areas of his life. When his teenage daughter dropped out of high school, he *disowned* her, refused to accept her irresponsible behavior. Another root of bitterness burrowed down. He even refused to speak to an aunt and uncle who had accepted that daughter into their home. And another root of bitterness burrowed down. His youngest son joined with his father, cutting off various family members any time they unwittingly offended. A whole lifetime stuck in the muck of resentment.

It gets into our genes

If there's one thing about those bitter roots, it's that getting rid of them requires a virtual excavation to get to the very bottom of their source. The tiniest remnant of that root can continue to sprout that judgment again and again. We will even begin to see our bitter root judgments sprouting in our children, in our children's children. The things that we don't deal with in our lifetime will be passed on to our descendants (possibly even biologically so), as Gabor Maté has noted: "Parenting, in short, is a dance of the generations. Whatever affected one generation, but has not been fully resolved will be passed on to the next."

It is evidenced by racial and even familial tensions in many nations. The family feud between the infamous Hatfields and McCoys—two families in the same southern region of the USA who battled over Civil War allegiances—ended in hatred, and eventually murder. The hostility between the Hutus and Tutsis of Rwanda can be traced back to the preference of the nations that colonized these areas for one tribe over another. Ancient wars between the Israelis and Arabs are traced back thousands of years to two half-brothers laying claim to the same inheritance. Loss, connected to injustice, can become the fuel that ignites and stokes the fires of generational anger, bitterness, and hatred.

To end the cycle of hatred set in motion by this kind of ancestral grievance seems impossible, but some unlikely demonstrations of sacrifice have produced surprising results. *Peace Child* is the story of Canadian Christian missionaries Don and Carol Richardson, who went into the cannibal tribes of New Guinea. They had begun working alternately with three warring Sawi tribal villages. The villagers had engaged in unabated hostilities and violence for decades. The Richardsons' kindness, medical help, practical care, and message of hope through God seemed to have made no impact.

After many years, concluding that their work was having little effect, the Richardsons determined to leave the region, and announced their decision to the Sawi villagers. Unbeknown to these missionaries, the tribes were silently being affected by the aid, the compassion, and the sacrifice of these two incomers. Village after village longed for Don and Carol to stay, and so they decided to take matters into their own hands.

In an effort to put their grievances to rest, adversarial tribal leaders gathered their people together for an ancient Sawi ceremony. As part of this ceremony, and in order to bring peace to the tribes, each tribe was required to take young children from their own tribes and exchange them with children of the opposing tribes—some literally putting their own sons right into the hands of a hated enemy. These children were to live the remainder of their lives in the homes of their family's foes. As Don Richardson observed, "If a man would actually give his own son to his enemies, that man could be trusted!" This unthinkable act had transformational repercussions, especially as it also suddenly gave context to the Richardsons' message of hope and faith (that is, Jesus was God's Peace Child, given to mankind as an offering to break down the wall of hostility between God and man). From that point on, peace reigned among the tribes and took root in the culture of the Sawi people.[37]

How does this translate to each of us in our anger and bitterness? Perhaps it is that we can provide that peace child. When we have suffered an injustice, if we give up our right to be embittered, to exact vengeance, to hate, and instead extend forgiveness, perhaps in this we offer our own peace child to end the war that rages inside us. If allowed to continue unchecked, unaddressed, this internal war can inflict silent, physical damage. We need to bring an end to it.

11

the science of grief

My hamstrings are tight—as far as I know they always have been—so it has typically been painful for me to do a hamstring stretch in a sports warm-up or in a dance class. I would wince and breathe heavily as my ballet instructor would push my back down further for a better hamstring stretch each ballet class, my entire being resisting the overwhelming urge to scream out in agony, "Okay! Stop! Stop! I can't do this anymore!" I readily understood, though, that the important objective in stretching is to maintain my composure long enough that the inflicted discipline would achieve an essential improvement in the mobility of my limbs. The compulsion to oppose the stretch had to be denied.

With this goal always in my mind, it was confounding to me that after my mom died, as I struggled to get my body back in dance condition, it was the hamstring stretch—with my legs extended straight, feet flexed, body bent in half over the length of my lower limbs—that suddenly triggered uncontrollable sobbing. Truly, I could not prevent the eruption of whimpering and unpredictable stream of tears, could not stop them from exerting their force on my composure. The torment of the stretch had strangely become so unbearable that I could no longer bring myself to submit to this important exercise. The physical pain was intense as always, but the emotional pain bothered me more. I was explaining this dilemma to my massage therapist one day, when he explained it simply: "Well, it's because your parasympathetic nervous system originates in the lower part of your spinal cord, right where your hamstrings also originate."

Now, what is the significance of the parasympathetic nervous system (PNS), you might ask? After we have experienced trauma or loss, it is our PNS that restores our *homeostasis*, our body's *normal functioning*

---

state. It brings our adrenal function back to normal, our heart rate to a healthy pace, digestion to its regular operation, our endorphins (the *feel-good* hormones) to an elevated state; in short, it works to stabilize our bodily functions after a crisis.

The PNS also stimulates our *tear glands*.[38] Strange, that the system that brings us back to a place of joy and a sense of well-being would activate tears, one of the main marks of sadness. What this affirms is that the awkward spill of weeping is actually necessary for releasing the positive physiological effects of the PNS, which helps restore our emotional equilibrium. You may have noticed that it can take more emotional energy to keep tears at bay than to surrender to their annoying assault. *Relieved* is what many feel when they are final able to discharge their pent-up tears. For some, a good cry is followed by feelings of joy, liberty, exhilaration.

Evoking emotions physically

So back to those hamstrings of mine ... It is apparent that tucked into the simple stretches of a dance class was a key to healing from loss. The pain of my tight hamstrings, now amplified by the pain in my heart, was causing tears to flow. Coupled with the heavy breathing of physical exertion, which also triggers my PNS, I was serving myself a great, healthy cocktail of restoration from grief. As a matter of fact, movement in general activates a mechanism for grieving.

American physical therapist Leia N. Ambra, in a study in which she interviewed numerous dance therapists who worked with adult women who were survivors of incest, discovered that dance/movement therapy can help these victims. Therapists reported that these traumatized women were able to verbalize their experiences, especially when the expression of their emotions was still threatening to unpack. They also revealed that dance was a helpful tool to enable a traumatized individual to access suppressed memories of a traumatic nature by engaging the body in a manner that can re-link memories through their kinesthetic/sensorimotor cues.[39]

It was this sort of connection that triggered Kerry's recollection of grief that she had never known was there. Kerry had come to our studio as an experienced dancer. She had spent many years and count-less hours in the demanding environment of competitive dance—punishing her body in the quest for increasing physical strength and flexibility; sacrificing her social life for an unfathomable number of hours in the studio; giving up her summers to train at elite dance academies. For her, too, the unspoken motto at the studios in the early years of her dance training had been to "Leave your emotions at the door." They had little use for what they perceived as the weak-ness and inconvenience of emotion. For those studios, dancers had to drive themselves in order to achieve excellence and perfection. Those weaknesses of emotion—fear, self-consciousness, apprehen-sion—had to be quashed in order to push to increasingly higher lev-els and this would result in a disconnection from those emotions.

When Kerry entered our studio, it was the first time that she had been told, "You are welcome to allow whatever feelings you are expe-riencing to spill out." For her, a whole other unexpected thing began to surface. Here in this relatively *safe* environment, she began to recall something she had never been consciously aware of before. Bit by bit, as her body was releasing itself into physical liberty, memories of an alarming sort were being recalled. Suddenly coming to the fore of her mind was the painful memory of being sexually abused as a child. The memories began to trickle in, and then flood in, as day by day her emotions bore witness to this unthinkable violation.

Dance became the release for her repressed feelings, and creating dance became her outlet for voicing the depression, the turmoil that was building up inside her. Expressions of anger, despair, hope-lessness, fear, made their way into the physical—she created dance movements that stomped and writhed and wilted and clutched—the non-verbal voice of her tumult. These were the beginning of a re-markable process of healing that has continued for many years.

A mounting internal agitation in the body can either create a toxic blend of turmoils or be uncorked in motion. It's why a person suf-fering emotional stress should go for a run or take an exercise/dance class. Not only does the physical exertion help to liberate the pent-up angst, it also releases endorphins, which in turn induce feelings of pleasure, happiness, and elation and facilitate relief from pain.[40]

Emotions' effect on our cells

In the area of human biology, we have begun to see the emergence of new fields of study that investigate the effect of our emotions on a physiological plane at the cellular level. A series of biochemical discoveries by Dr. Candace Pert,[41 42] renowned neuroscientist and former chief of biochemistry at the National Institutes of Health (NIH) in the USA, and Dr. Bruce Lipton, cellular biologist specializing in genes and DNA, among others, have led to whole new areas of research called *psychoneuroimmunology* and *epigenetics*, which look at the interrelationships between our mental, emotional, and physical aspects.

Previously, it had been presumed that our emotional brain, the limbic system (hypothalamus, hippocampus, amygdala), controlled most of what we experience as emotion. These areas have always been thought to be the initiators of emotion, learning, memory, and motivation, but recent studies have shown that there is a pervasive cellular component. The assumption had always been that our body's emotional system functioned independently of our physiological systems, but based on the research of Dr. Pert, we now understand that there are *molecules of emotion*. Pert discovered that the chemical compounds called peptides, which primarily function as signaling molecules throughout the body, are released in every part of our physical being and can uniquely become effectual in the communication between body and emotions.

Dr. Pert proposed the notion of a molecule of emotion, but we need to recall our high school biology in order to understand this concept—and I will attempt to keep it simple for those of us who aren't scientifically inclined. The communication of our emotions (mood and behavior) happens via chemical compounds called *neuropeptides*, which are secreted by the brain and bond to the receptors on the surface of the cells throughout our body. They were traditionally believed to be present only in the emotional brain, but it is now known they are found in any place in the body that is responsible for any one of our five senses.

Dr. Pert's amazing discovery was that these neuropeptides were "signaling cancer cells [via their receptors] to grow and metastasize to different parts of the body." It was further revealed that they join with the immune system, the brain, and the glands as "a network of communication between brain and body, probably representing the biochemical substrate of emotion." In other words, they had uncovered that the information mechanism used to convey emotion in a person (that is, *neuropeptides* from the emotional brain) also had the ability to affect a person's physical health.

Bodies as a cask of grief

There is no denying that grief has a definitive impact on our bodies—it leaves a lump in the throat; it produces a tightness in the chest; it causes a weakness in the limbs; it suppresses the appetite. We have all witnessed it, all experienced it. And yet, throughout the centuries, scientists, physicians, even psychiatrists have struggled to prove the mind-body connection as it relates to our emotions.

Our bodies demonstrate the repercussions of losses ungrieved in countless ways, and psychologists have determined that there are a number of physical effects arising from grief: sleep difficulties, poor appetite or overeating, shakiness or trembling, listlessness, disorientation, migraines or headaches, dizziness, dry mouth, crying, numbness, shortness of breath, exhaustion, increased arthritis symptoms.

In his book *The Wounded Heart*, Dr. Dan Allender addresses the many challenges faced by adults who were victims of childhood sexual abuse, one form of grief. Dr. Allender has observed that, although some of his patients would like to believe that they just got over the trauma of their abuse and that it no longer affects them, their physical condition says otherwise. He has observed that it has affected their physical health, their behavior, their emotional state, and their spiritual well-being (that is, body, soul, and spirit). He notes that "ulcers, intestinal problems, lower backaches, stiff neck, tight jaw and chronic headaches" are common among the sexual abuse victims he counsels. These grief symptoms connected to sexual abuse suggest that ungrieved loss lingers in us in a physiological way until it can be dealt with, healed, in an emotional way.[43]

Dr. Carol Burckhardt, who works extensively with people who have fibromyalgia, has discovered that her patients' initial symptoms are also similar to the physical effects of grief—fatigue, sleep disturbances, digestive abnormalities, joint stiffness, numbness. But what grief might be connected to this physiological affect? She has also discovered that sexual abuse is a common experience in the lives of those who have fibromyalgia.[44 45]

Some medical professionals are now taking note and are more frequently acknowledging the possibility of emotional connections to bodily ailments. Caroline, whose parents divorced while she was still in elementary school, developed an unusual response to the emotional duress emanating from her family's domestic strife. She was stricken with a crippling arthritis in her hands—an extremely uncommon ailment for a child so young. But her doctor understood the possible connection to her life circumstances. Another doctor might have simply accepted this ailment and its crippling effects at face-value and prescribed pain relievers or anti-inflammatories, but her very wise physician suggested something different. He proposed that she take up playing the piano in an effort to keep the finger joints lubricated and mobilized, perhaps staving off the effects of the arthritis. This *dancing with the hands* proved to be a miraculous therapy. The pain and stiffness soon disappeared as she began to play regularly.

To move further on this idea and look at dance and its impact on the physiological aftereffects of stress, I pause to mention again the role of *endorphins*. Endorphins are key hormones that are released when a physical activity such as dance is engaged in. Dr. Howard Kosterlitz, an award-winning biologist, famously discovered that when the digestive tract is being provoked by a stressful stimulus, if endorphins are released, they can actually halt the stress-related activation of the digestive tract. In other words, when endorphins are released by such physical pursuits as dancing, this activity can decrease the physiological turmoil (digestive abnormalities in this example) provoked by the stress of grief.[46]

Grief at the cellular level

That the connection between emotions and physiological health can be definitively linked is still a relatively new development, but the historic discovery of the multitude of orphans in the orphanages of Romania in 1989 unmistakably established this mind-body interplay.[47]

Visitors to the disheveled, gloomy, dank buildings struggled to shake the smothering realization that in the rows of battered cribs, in a room thick with the stench of urine and excrement, under flimsy and tattered linens, lay babies and young children ... dozens and dozens of them in wall-to-wall crib-cages. The greatest shock to these Western visitors was the fact that all these children were in various states of emotional distress, physical atrophy, and overall deterioration. Many shrieked incessantly in dismay, others had ceased to cry. They had learned early in their lives that crying would produce no response, no attention, no care. This was Ceausescu's Romania in 1989. When the dictator's government fell and he was executed, the orphanages, housing tens of thousands of the nation's abandoned children, became the focus of inspection, and outrage, from the outside world.

Most notable to observers was that these young ones, many of them older than their emaciated frames indicated, had suffered abuse and neglect to the degree that a great number of them had developed a confounding collection of psychological and *physical* anomalies—stunted growth, deteriorating flesh, tuberculosis, crossed eyes, an inability to walk or talk, rocking, self-harm. The main common deficiency beyond sufficient nutrition and adequate hygiene—which, it was agreed, could not adequately explain most of the physical afflictions—was simply love and care. An unspeakable evil had been inflicted on these children when their families had abandoned them to these state-run orphanages—poverty and Ceausescu's reproductive policies, which limited the number of children per family, left many parents with no choice but to surrender their children.

The whole scene attracted the professional attention of doctors and psychologists from far and wide. There was certainly a presumption

that a child in these conditions would exhibit emotional detach-
ment, rocking, and self-comfort, for example, but how did a lack of
love and care so distort the physical development of a child? The
answer seemed to lie in that elusive link between the mind and the
body. Although psychology and medical professionals might intuitively conclude that there is a connection between negative, harmful
emotions and their impact on our bodies, the correlation has to
date defied definition.[48]

The reasons for this lie in our Western medical practice. Doctors
are, for the most part, trained to treat symptoms and do not generally delve into illness prevention. They will prescribe pills, treatments,
and the like, but will rarely probe into the personal or emotional
lives of their patients—until the early 21st century, there was little
recognized scientific evidence to prove that there was any connection between our minds/emotions and our physical health.

Century after century, the belief that an individual's physical health
was independent of his or her emotional health has so dominated
medical thought that there has even been open contempt for anyone
who would dare to claim that a person's physical well-being is the
sum of its internal and external influences. That mindset is in the
process of shifting. In relevant areas of medical science, the effect of
emotions (and for our purposes, grief) at the cellular level are being
exposed, and so contributing to our understanding of the mind-
body connection. Here I will consider discoveries about the functioning of our cells during chronic stress/grief, and discussing how
they can actually become sick. We will first uncover how emotions
can affect our cells; then we will look at how our cells can adapt
themselves to adjust to their stressful environment, altering their
configuration in the process; and finally we will take a look at the
impact of emotions on physical recovery.

Uncovering the truth

Dr. Gabor Maté has written about the hurdles faced by those seeking
to address the idea of a mind-body connection:

Many doctors over the centuries came to understand that

emotions are deeply implicated in the causation of illness or in the restoration of health. They did research, wrote books and challenged the reigning medical ideology, but repeatedly their ideas, explorations and insights vanished in a sort of medical Bermuda Triangle. The understanding of the mind-body connection achieved by previous generations of doctors and scientists disappeared without a trace, as if it had never seen daylight.

His conclusion regarding the consequences for our overall health is:

> That lost capacity for physical and emotional self-awareness is at the root of much of the stress that chronically debilitates health and prepares the ground for disease.[49]

He further observes that it will likely be the lay public who will most effectively bring the mind-body connection to light for two reasons: they are not restricted by the confines of traditional scientific understanding and they intuitively understand that the human being is holistic in its mind-body connection. However, it would appear that there is a gradual turning of the tide on this subject in the medical arena.

Cells alter themselves

As we look at the cell on an even more active level, it is apparent that our emotions are constantly adjusting the internal environment of the cell. Dr. Bruce Lipton, well-known cell biologist in the area of *epigenetics*, contends that how we perceive the world around us has a critical impact on our cells. He suggests that our genes are constantly being affected not only by changes in our environment but also by our perceptions of our environment.[50]

Where it used to be understood that genes were set, that they affected various manifestations of illnesses, behaviors, and appearances, and that mutations in those genes were random, we now know that there is a phenomenon called adaptive mutations. If there is a constant sense of danger, fear, depression, the cells respond accordingly, adapting their internal environment by mutating their normal configuration and functionality to suit this sustained state of peril.

In the case of grief, a person who has not adequately dealt with the various aspects of their loss will continue to perceive the world around them as hopeless, threatening, perhaps even terrifying. They may remain in a perpetual state of anxiety, victimization, anger—and their body will begin to respond in a protective manner. Crisis, loss, stress all trigger in the body an overall emergency response: the immune system begins to shut down; cells begin to inhibit growth and development in order to protect themselves; the activity of the cell is adjusted to adapt to the external environment (that is, crisis).[51][52] This emergency response is the fight or flight instinct which is triggered by any perception of danger. It is intended to give us the ability to escape, to protect against, to battle against whatever threatening circumstance is perceived. Although this *fight* or *flight* response is meant to be quick, powerful, and brief, if it persists, the cells will begin to become ineffective in fighting illness, in regenerating healthy cells, in working in the manner for which they are designed.

Typically, peptides communicate with the cell's function at the receptor site on the surface of each cell somewhat like a lock and key. A peptide (the key) will connect with the cell at its unique site (the lock) and activate the cell to carry out its particular function.[53] Those peptides also activate a cell's return to homeostasis, its normal state, after it has coped with a crisis (again, for our discussion, the crisis would be loss and grief). But when a state of crisis is prolonged, this communication via the peptides (or lack thereof) at the cell surface will actually begin to produce changes within the cell that are adaptations to what is now perceived as a negative environment created by the aggravated emotions. The cell essentially becomes sick because of our emotional state.

Further, through his experiments, Dr. Lipton could show that a sick cell could be taken from an ill individual in a specific external environment and be placed in a normal (that is, healthy) body in the same external environment and it would thrive—it would change its genetic expression to become healthy.[54] That same cell put back into the sick person will begin to get sick again. In other words, the genetic code of the cell was being actively adjusted in response to the internal environment. This adjustment, he contends, is caused by our emotional perception or belief (this can include both real circumstances taking place and also an individual's attitudes toward those circumstances).

Bodies communicating with our minds

When the stress of grief goes underground for a long period of time, it can also start to become *ineffective in alerting* us to situations of emotional overload or danger. The normal emotional response triggered through our brains and limbic system in times of emotional threat can get numbed to typical cues that let us know that it's time to stop, to pull back, to protect. This could put us at great risk were it not for a remarkable secondary signaling system: our body.

Studies, and in particular studies with people who have irritable bowel syndrome (IBS), have demonstrated that the digestive system can actually take over emotional responses when the brain and limbic systems get shut down. In a study by Dr. Howard Mertz,[55] renowned gastroenterologist and author, it was demonstrated that when people with IBS are confronted with a painful stimulus in the bowel (a small balloon inflated in the region), their anterior cingulate cortex (ACC)[56] would spontaneously be triggered (neural signals coming from the bowel). What is the significance of these areas of the brain? Not only do they process pain, but they also process emotion (fear, anxiety, anger).

It has long been accepted that our emotions (activated in the ACC region of our brains) can trigger our digestive tract (stomach, intestine, bowel ...), but what is new in this study (and other similar studies) is that we are now seeing *the digestive tract* (the bowel in this case), *triggering the emotional centers* (note that this does not happen to the same degree in those who do not have IBS, though it is unclear why). Dr. Maté has suggested that the bowels were signaling the brain to arouse emotion, in times or situations of distress, when the emotions have shut down.[57]

What this means is that our digestive system can become a substitute emotions activator if our emotions have been numbed by pain or trauma. Regarding our discussion about pain and loss, our digestive system will respond to the fear, the danger triggered by the continuous state of turmoil, and then stimulate the brain (which may have been numbed by the trauma) to feel the required emotions. Astounding!

Dancing as body-soul therapy

How does dance fit into all this? First of all, let me note the connection between chronic stress (incomplete grieving of a loss can place an individual in a state of chronic stress) and memory loss/dementia. In brief, research shows that stress hormones damage the memory center of the brain (the hippocampus), causing memory loss,[58] which can lead to dementia. In other words, that constant barrage of stressful emotions triggers a continual release of hormones that can actually jeopardize the survival of brain cells, *it can kill brain cells.*[59][60]

With this in mind, I turn to a dramatic study[61] by researchers at the Albert Einstein College in New York. In this study, published in 2003, a group of seniors were observed over a period of twenty-one years and assessed in terms of incidences of dementia and Alzheimer's in conjunction with various recreational activities. The results of this study were largely unexpected by the researchers and have become the source of much discussion and hypothesizing, particularly because they involve dancing.

The study focused on determining whether certain recreational activities would decrease the incidence of memory loss/dementia/Alzheimer's (recall that ungrieved loss can also result in memory loss/dementia, or did you forget?). Cognitive pursuits such as doing crossword puzzles, playing cards, reading, creative writing, playing musical instruments were looked at, as were physical activities such as golfing, walking, cycling, playing tennis, dancing, swimming, doing housework, etc. The results were tabulated according to each activity's percentage likelihood of reducing the risk of memory loss/dementia.

Notably, some of the mental activities apparently decreased the risk, though this seemed contingent on the level of creative thinking required by the activity. But among the great surprises of the study was that virtually none of the physical activities produced any evident change in the risk of dementia—with one exception. The summary of a few of the results are below:

- Playing golf: 0% reduced risk of dementia
- Doing crossword puzzles at least four days a week: 47% reduced risk
- Reading: 35% reduced risk
- Cycling and swimming: 0% reduced risk
- Dancing: 76% reduced risk

Remarkably, dancing was the only physical activity that resulted in a reduced risk of dementia, and was even more effective than the most risk-reducing mental activity! So, what can be gleaned from these surprising conclusions? Researchers and critics have also produced three distinct speculations regarding the results:

1. The learning of dance steps creates *new neural pathways*.

2. Dance *stimulates creativity*, which evokes the will to live and also creates new neural pathways.

3. Dance *releases endorphins*, which help to improve memory, alleviate pain, and restore a sense of well-being.

Neural pathways are the way all information flows through our brains. What the medical community has always understood about dementia is that, as the illness progresses, the neural pathways begin to shut down one by one. Activities that require single neural pathways (that is, they use repetitive movements)—golfing, cycling, swimming, for example—will have the least effect on the generation of new neural activity in the brain. Activities that require logical thinking, snap decision-making, or creative processing constantly develop new neural pathways.

As memory loss progresses and existing neural pathways are shut down, the more mentally demanding pursuits are continuously generating alternative pathways to preserve memory and mental capabilities. Dancing requires the execution of numerous new combinations of steps and often requires quick decisions, direction changes, and creative solutions, constantly activating new neural pathways.[62]

Add to this the creative aspect[63] of dance: freely creating your own steps; creatively learning or interpreting new steps; creatively executing combinations of steps with a partner. As noted in Chapter 6, biochemist Dr. Ana Aslan[64] has mentioned that creativity aids the recovery of the body and its balance after grief because it is one aspect of the will to live and therefore facilitates the body's response to degenerating illnesses. But to prod further, functionally speaking, creative thinking acts as a rerouter around blocked neural pathways that result from the progressive deterioration of memory as connected to chronic grief. Picture a road blocked for construction and the detour signs that redirect you on a different path through the city. Creative thinking provides many alternative avenues of mental processing so that any obstructions, due to failing neural pathways, can be effectively circumvented. Dance, especially dance of a creative, spontaneous and freestyling sort, creates multiple new alternative routes around blocked neural pathways.

Laughing ourselves to health

So, what is to become of us when the effects of grief linger? Does our health need to be forever altered? Thankfully, the answer is "no." Just as we have emotional mechanisms that can provoke illness, we equally have emotional mechanisms that can encourage health.

In an unlikely experiment by renowned journalist and political activist Norman Cousins,[65] it was demonstrated that his emotional health could change the course of his physical health. Cousins was diagnosed with ankylosing spondylitis, a potentially life-threatening illness with no cure. Although he cites that his physical state was likely due to a combination of factors, including stressful circumstances and an ingestion of an unusually high quantity of truck and airplane exhaust while traveling in the USSR during the Cold War era, he was intent on reversing his dire prognosis. Cousins checked himself into a hotel with a collection of funny videos, humorous readings, and a daily dose of Vitamin C, believing that the release of endorphins and the restorative properties of the vitamin would produce a physical recovery. He claims from his own observations in his book *Anatomy of an Illness: As Perceived by the Patient* that he literally laughed himself into good health. Having deduced from his own study that the release of *endorphins*, through the constant experience of joy, would enable his body to heal itself, he set out on his personal health experiment, ultimately confounding the medical community. Doctors had concluded that his illness was irreversibly degenerative, but the symptoms of the disease completely disappeared.

Endorphins are neuropeptide neurotransmitters that are responsible for restoring the body to a condition of normal health after a period of illness, stress, or crisis. As mentioned previously, endorphins are released through laughter, affection, joyful activities, physical exercise, and dance; they are responsible for making us feel good and even for reducing physical pain. When we are under stress or emotional duress, as in times of grief, there is a decreased release of endorphins to our cells—and the cells become less receptive to the endorphins.

In the case of our Romanian orphans, with little or no stimulation whatsoever and especially little social interaction that would encourage the release of endorphins (no laughter, no affection, no joy, no dancing), their little bodies would have been seriously deprived of these essential restorative neuropeptides. Bit by bit, the cells of their bodies would begin to deteriorate, weaken, cease to function effectively, even die, due to the lack of endorphins resulting from inadequate love and care.

There are so many applications for these discoveries, but that is beyond the scope of this book. Suffice it to say that completing our process of grieving is an essential goal for the sake of not only our emotional health, but also our physical health.

Dancing and the will to live

To return to the study on activities and their effect on the development of dementia, dance, when compared to the other dementia-reducing activities in the study, has an added feature: the release of endorphins. Since endorphins aid in recovery from stress, crisis, and trauma, their release is essential to compensate for the detrimental effects of stress hormones, relieving pain and even triggering a sense of pleasure in the process.

Endorphins become crucial in renovating the wreck of the being ravaged by grief.[66] The exhilaration, joy, even laughter released when a physical activity like dance is engaged in creates in the body a powerful restorative compound that can rebuild body and soul.

I know what gets unleashed when people begin to dance: joy. Many times I have experienced the extraordinary reaction when my husband, the musician, strikes up a song and encourages a whole crowd of strangers to circle dance (the last time was with tens of thousands on the streets of our city). Whenever I watch these unsuspecting participants grab the hand of the person next to them and begin to dance, circling left, then circling right, then into the middle with a yell, there is never anything but smiles (and laughter and glee!) on the faces of those participating. Joy is instantaneous with dance, and joy (that is, endorphins) facilitates the body's ability to heal itself.

We can't help but heal quicker, think better, and shake ourselves free from the pain of grief simply by choosing to dance.

12

grieving chronic illness and multiple losses

Our bodies are remarkable. Their ability to restore and recover even after unimaginable emotional devastation is nothing short of miraculous. But there are times when our bodies are unable to recover—sometimes chronic illness is not followed by restoration. In such circumstances, our bodies suddenly become the source of our grief.

I met my friend Collette the summer that I moved to the west coast. She was newly engaged to Peter, and the two of them seemed to me the most gracious and vibrant characters I had ever met, pouring love over everyone around them. Though she was a little older than me, we were soon friends. What most drew me to this petite beauty was that she had a way of experiencing life as a constant dialogue to be sorted through, processed, and passed on.

In the last few years, we have spent less and less time together, but Collette has consistently managed to contact me at divinely appointed times when I was facing personal life challenges. She would always start with, "I'm not sure why I am calling, but I've been thinking about you all day and had to contact you." She called when Russ and I were going through a financial crisis, when my youngest daughter got sick, when I needed some outside wisdom to help me make an important decision, when my mother died. Her insight and comfort have always been exactly what I needed in the moment. Through the years, though, one of the main things we have shared is grief—though much of it was initially hers. At that time I was not yet versed in loss, and thus, regrettably, offered feeble support for the difficulties that she was facing emotionally, but I did my best to encourage and comfort her, keeping my heart open to listen.

Collette's back story is replete with continual overcoming. Her best friend, Eden, developed leukemia and died while still in her twenties. Collette stayed with her and cared for her throughout her illness. When Collette's daughter, her second child, was born with a genetic syndrome requiring constant medical interventions and demanding years of regular hospital visits, our heroine hunkered down and gave exceptional care. Collette's fourth child arrived via international adoption and experienced some of the challenges of identity that adopted children often face. Collette and Peter bore those trials with strength but experienced them deeply, emotionally.

Several years after her fourth child arrived, a precious baby boy, a foster child, joined their ranks. The couple of weeks he was to be with them evolved into a couple of years, and as the heart bonds grew increasingly strong, he became *their* little boy. Although Collette was determined to adopt him, the government intervened and he was adopted by another family. Collette was heartbroken.

When Collette was in her thirties, her biggest loss hit with unexpected force: *chronic illness*. Collette had already weathered more challenges than anyone deserves, but this new one brought with it an unending series of losses, physical inabilities that constantly shifted and changed, presenting her daily with new turmoil, new challenges. Her diagnosis, multiple sclerosis, gave rise to a grief incomparable to any she had experienced to date.

A whole other set of grieving skills is required for this sort of loss because of its relentless assault on a person's physical stability. MS, terminal cancer, HIV/AIDS, ALS, and other serious illnesses are prison sentences from which, to date, there is unlikely parole. There is no getting around the daily confrontation with grief when a single *death* has triggered a cascade of further fatalities. Chronic illness is such death. Each day seems lacerated by yet another undeserved lash on the back of vitality, a slow, somatic erosion. It is water cupped in the hands of a child; hope drains through unseen gaps.

A new type of loss

For Collette, it began as numbness in her feet, as though she had left them in icy cold water for too long. It was strange, but really not much to bother about. When the sensation continued, though, she underwent a battery of tests and was finally diagnosed with MS. The symptoms were not immediately concerning: a bit of fatigue, some tingling in her limbs, a few more clumsy stumbles than usual, but little more. A busy mom and nurse, she carried on as normal for the next few years, aware of only slightly peculiar symptoms that seemed to come and go with each year.

When I finally connected with Collette again, it had been a few years since I had actually seen her, and so I was not quite up to speed with the progression of her illness. I was taken aback by her noticeable limp and now regular use of a cane. Her lovely banter and jovial demeanor were still a constant, but it was apparent that her physical well-being was taking a beating. The MS had now begun to progress in a manner that had inflicted a more brutal attack on her daily activities: severe exhaustion; loss of muscle strength; constant bladder problems; permanently numbed body parts; an increasing inability to walk. It was with the degeneration of her body that she began to enter a whole new phase of grieving.

As still a relatively young woman—one who loved to hike, cycle, and snowboard—the inescapable advancement of her disease, with its inevitable fate, bestowed on her an unimaginable despair. When she began to consider a wheelchair, her emotions began to dive.

Being a nurse, she was well aware of what could happen in the later stages of her illness and of what a wheelchair would mean: she may, at some point, never walk again. This dire prospect began to pummel her emotions. Almost daily, she found herself constantly on the verge of tears. Every personal conversation stoked the rising flames of distress. The persistent reminders of her escalating losses fed her sorrow. What was to become of her in a progressive state of incapacity? Of inability? Of physical disintegration? Someday she wouldn't be able to feed or clothe herself, enjoy a walk, leave her house. Unexpected floods of tears, an undertow of loss and sadness, laid siege to her day after struggling day.

This is a prison whose walls draw in closer day by day, hour by hour.

The movement of their progression is barely noticeable, but the sense of the world closing in—time and space diminishing, the ability to live narrowing—is undeniable. The suffocating knowledge of a future with no reprieve in sight had bagged her and dragged her away. She was overwhelmed by grief.

It was a thoughtful friend, one who had witnessed Collette's exponential loss and tears, who finally, kindly, confronted her. "Collette, I think it's time for you to stop focusing on what you have lost and start being thankful for what you had the privilege of enjoying while you had it." A bold statement. And one that might seem a little cruel to the rest of us. But for Collette, who had been taking the time to mourn through her losses during the previous weeks and years, this well-intentioned prodding was just what she needed. The change in perspective seemed to give her a new lease on life.

Truly, she had enjoyed enormous gifts through her lifetime: an amazing husband, years of fantastic physical abilities, wonderful children who have now become loving young adults, enormous opportunities to make a difference in the lives of many people whom she had mentored and cared for. As she revisited and reviewed the gifts that had filled her life, the sorrow was almost immediately replaced with a confidence and expectancy. It was a peace she had never before experienced.

Losing and gaining

For me, Collette has always been an unbelievable blessing. Her perspective is invariably one of wisdom, faith, direction, and encouragement. She is one who lets the tears stream when they come. She really can't hold them back, ever. I sense that this is the fruit of all her life challenges. Her life trials have given her the ability to courageously go to the place of pain, confront it, and then allow the full magnitude of the loss to course through her because *it is in the place of your pain that healing can come.* I am thankful that she has been generous in sharing this gift.

But this is likely not what you want to hear when you have suddenly been diagnosed with a progressive or chronic illness. It does not help to hear that it will *build character* or that *something good will come out of this, just wait and see*. All you can feel is pain, regret, fear, anger, guilt. It's difficult to shake the constant questioning: *Why did this have to happen to me?* Or worse, *what could I have done differently to prevent this from happening?* So, yes, it's helpful to let the tears come, to allow the grief to grip your being, permitting the sorrow to flood through, just as Collette did.

Let me make another note as well. With all the scientific revelations surfacing about the body-mind connection, as noted in the previous chapter, you might be tempted to point to all the *should haves: I should have taken better care of my body; I should have dealt with my stress better; I should have detected this sooner*. At this point it is important resist guilt, to not *should* on yourself but to embrace, or at least face, the disappointments brought by this life change. The grief is as grueling as the physical symptoms. It represents continuous, multiple losses and requires much grace and compassion—especially from you to yourself.

The resulting soul ache cannot be ignored or smoothed over, lest despair grow below the surface. Tears are again the welcome healer of this life sentence. Chronic illness does, for certain, need to be acknowledged for its unsightly affliction, but perhaps, I would add, also for its unpredictable beauty. Some have profoundly understood this.

Morrie Schwartz was a professor of sociology whose slow degeneration in the grip of ALS (also known as Lou Gehrig's disease) was famously documented by his former student Mitch Albom in the book *Tuesdays with Morrie*.[67] It is a fascinating look at the progression of grieving chronic illness through the eyes of one who chooses to experience life with utter vulnerability and exceptional joy. Morrie holds back none of the agony, confessing to weeping most mornings, but surprisingly, he extracts more gratitude for life in the midst of his illness than one might expect.

At one point, Morrie mentions the key to what he seemed to be learning from his disease: "The most important thing in life is to learn how to give out love, and to let it come in." When a person becomes imprisoned by an illness, a whole other appreciation for life and for love arises.

In our busy and competent periods of life, we can become most ungrateful: *this project didn't work out the way I wanted; that person doesn't love me the way they should; I didn't get what I expected.* When our expectations are stripped away by the limiting circumstances of an illness, we actually have an opportunity to live life with a greater sense of wonder and thankfulness.

All is not lost

There is a unique retrospective that comes with chronic illness and that has the ability to deepen life experience in ways few can predict. Chronic illness, particularly one that has the potential to end in premature loss of life as Morrie's did, is a sudden death with the gift of added time. Time to reflect on, and reckon with, life and relationships. Consistently throughout *Tuesdays* we watch a young man (Mitch) develop a growing sense of his own soul poverty compared to the soul treasure that Morrie seems to have dug up in his advance toward death.

And for some, a terminal illness has provided an unexpected reckoning.

Tom had always been a sarcastic guy. His quick wit, social reclusiveness, and persistent drinking habit happened to be secretly masking a growing mound of self-hatred. His gracious wife was a constant mediator, cushioning life around Tom so that his razor-sharp wit would be less inclined to lacerate others, but it rarely worked. This abrasive young man would always manage to find something to tactlessly poke at. It was an inescapable vicious cycle that even Tom recognized.

One day he had offered a careless comment, like a prayer, pleading, "God, can you help me to become a more patient and kind man, husband, father?" There seemed to be an almost immediate response just months later: cancer (a little disclaimer here—I do not believe that cancer is a punishment from God, but Tom was convinced of a divine connection between his diagnosis and its timing). His diagnosis was dire and his progression toward death was shockingly swift, but a most notable miracle of healing began to appear in the area of his caustic words. Almost overnight, as his gratitude for his family and his life began to increase, his cynicism, dissatisfaction, and expectation began to decrease. By the time his mortal life had ended, he had become the gracious and loving man he had longed to be.

When illness affects us, perspective can be hammered out and peace can be wrought with a *bigger picture* outlook—life, eternity, love ... this is life-giving.

13

grieving a child with a
chronic illness

As an adult, it is one thing to begin to deal with the tumult of your own chronic illness, but let me assure you, it is nothing compared to the grief a parent experiences when their child is suddenly diagnosed with a chronic illness. Numerous bodily fatalities, or threats of death, emanating from a single life event are the daily crises that face the family of a chronically ill child. The powerlessness created by the ever-changing health dilemmas of your own child can torment a parent's sanity. The need to retain hope for the sake of the child while battling a nagging sense of helplessness can produce a conflicted grief.

I have one rather lengthy story that I felt needed to be told in its entirety. I trust it will clearly show the scope of the grief of those involved, the process of their grieving, and the victories of a quite remarkable journey.

Rob and Janet have always been one of the coolest, hippest couples I know. It was therefore not surprising to me that on the heels of their very early marriage, they found themselves teaching outdoor education and humanities to Saudi Arabian princes and princesses at an elite summer school in Switzerland. It was a dream job. Young in years and even younger in appearance, these two exemplified the untethered, adventuring, international lifestyle my old, settled, married friends and I had always envied. But just into the first year of their three-year contract, they had a sudden kick in their carefree pants: Janet was pregnant.

As non-citizens of Switzerland, the cost of Swiss medical care was completely out of reach for them, so they made a firm decision to return to Canada to deliver the baby. The pregnancy was relatively uneventful, and Janet was intent on ensuring, like many of her contemporaries, that she would have a natural delivery (that is, no drugs, no cesarean). Even at 37 weeks, when a small tear in the placenta caused the doctor to send her in for an ultrasound, there still didn't seem to be any problems, and she was left to go another few weeks with the hope of a natural birth. Unfortunately, at 42 weeks, with the baby overdue, the doctor finally made the decision to induce Janet.

The progression of labor was fairly typical, but her body was resisting dilation, so the doctor slowed the process to give Janet time to dilate. Janet and Rob napped awhile, taking the opportunity to rest when they could, when suddenly the nurses burst into the room in a panic: "The baby's heart rate is dipping!" The baby's heart monitor was indicating a rapid decline that they knew was dire. The medical staff executed a series of rushed treatments and the infant's heart rate swiftly returned to normal. But it was immediately evident that they would need to do a c-section, and soon. Unfortunately, there were already three other women in need of emergency cesareans—Janet would have to wait. Nine hours later, they finally wheeled her into the operating room, and after a bit of tugging and wrestling (the baby was firmly pressed into the pelvis), a beautiful tiny girl, Jordan, was delivered. Healthy by all initial appearances, but appearances can be deceptive.

Clear clues

Jordan was a quiet baby—she didn't even cry at birth. "She's just exhausted," they had said, and so Janet chose not to be concerned. Although Janet also noted that Jordan had a slightly large head, there didn't seem to be anything uncommon about her diminutive darling. That is, for the first five months. But a trip to Ireland for a wedding suddenly provoked a couple of concerns. There was one night when she had screamed for three hours—this baby who never made a peep. Upon their return to Canada, Janet had said to her doctor, "The Irish people were quite rude. They kept saying that my baby had a huge head." She giggled. "I mean, it's large, but I had a large head as a baby ..." She had deliberately overlooked a strange incident in Ireland when she had attempted to put a hat on Jordan and it didn't fit, although it had fit the day before. She had dismissed it with "Must've shrunk."

"We'll just measure that head," the doctor consoled her. She measured once, twice, three times ... She brought in a nurse and she measured ... The doctor was suddenly quite somber. She reassured Janet that she might be wrong, but by her measurements, Jordan's head had grown 6 cm since their last visit. It should have only grown 0.5 cm in that time. Within minutes, baby Jordan was whisked off for an ultrasound. The scan revealed the shocking evidence that this precious 5½-month-old baby girl had water on the brain, a condition called hydrocephalus. If not treated, it was a serious, indeed life-threatening, condition. It was determined that she would need an MRI as soon as possible, but there was a six-month wait. Panic began to rise.

Rob's dad had connections with a radiologist in another town that was just a quick flight away. "If you can fly them up here immediately," the radiologist had said, "I have an MRI machine sitting empty. I could see them tomorrow morning."

Without hesitation, Janet hopped on a plane that very day and flew with little Jordan to that northern Ontario town. The MRI completed, she and the radiologist looked together at the scans. They were dumbfounded. Neither of them were prepared for what they were about to see.

As they looked at the image, Janet, who has a background in physiology, suddenly burst out with, "I don't understand. Where is her brain?" She could see on the scan a vast dark area and a tiny rim of light around the edge. The radiologist pointed to the narrow light area around the outside, and Janet's eyes widened. Silence was their only response as the unbelievable reality began to sink in.

"Can you tell me," the radiologist prodded, "is she sitting up, making eye contact, smiling and clapping [the typical milestones for her age]?"

"Yes," Janet had confidently affirmed.

It didn't make any sense, he said. A child with such a meager amount of brain mass is typically an entirely nonfunctional human being. He continued, commenting that she also didn't have a vermis and that a vermis is necessary for the development of motor skills. He quickly informed Janet that children who are missing a vermis generally lie on the floor, incapacitated and blind, with no quality of life. Why was Jordan functioning normally?

"Has this baby been dropped on her head?" he continued.

"Absolutely not," Janet assured him (she confesses, laughing now, that she would not be able to answer so certainly about any of her subsequent babies, but with this one she could).

Distressed, he decisively concluded that this baby had had a massive hemorrhage and that she needed surgery—now!

The day of decision

Janet flew back home engulfed in tears and unbridled despair, her jovial baby flirting throughout the trip with the gentleman in the seat behind them. And yet, when she returned to the original neural surgeon, he was openly irritated that she had gone behind his back for an MRI. Defiantly, he determined that he would make her wait! But Janet knew that the radiologist had been insistent that this baby could not wait even two weeks. Jordan needed surgery immediately.

Rob and Janet pleaded with the neural surgeon, insisting that it was a matter of life and death, but he would not budge. His response was dismissive: "Everybody thinks their child's problems are urgent."

Janet was undone and hopeless. But again, there was a providential contact in the picture. A friend knew the surgeon's wife, and, long story short, they suddenly had an appointment for surgery two days hence. But now came the reality check: the chances of Jordan sur-viving the surgery were just 50-50, with an additional possibility that she would end up in a wheelchair for life. Rob and Janet knew they had to go ahead with the surgery, but Janet began to grapple with the terrifying nearness of her daughter's mortality and the awful realization that the outcome was, for this moment, entirely in their hands. How could she risk losing her? She loved her too much!

It was Rob, a young man of just 22, who responded with wisdom to Janet's fears. "We have a choice to raise this child in a bubble, to seal her off from the rest of the world, to put a helmet on her and walk around as though she is fragile and sick, or we have a choice to raise her and empower her to be the person that she can be. I refuse to believe that she will be a vegetable ... You're a worrier ... You have to choose what you are going to do."

True, she had always been a worrier—about small things, about big things—fear constantly plaguing her peace. The whole night before the surgery, Janet wrestled with her humanity, with her desire to raise her daughter in a bubble, with her faith ("God, where are you in all of this?!"). She took stock of the physical peculiarities Jordan might have: the tiny arm, the limp, the shaved head. It was all so unfair and painful and horrible!

How could she have let this happen? And how could she subject her daughter to more pain in life? Guilt lurked in the shadows of her agitated mind. Guilt that she hadn't asked more questions of the ultrasound technician while Jordan was still in utero. Guilt that she hadn't noticed things were not quite right when she was first born. Guilt that she could see now that there had been a dozen signs and symptoms before and after her birth that she had dismissed. And now it was too late. As the night wore on, she wrestled with her emotions. There seemed to be no answer, no hope.

But somewhere in the night a single thought alighted, a resignation settled in, and her tempest finally fizzled out. Unexpectedly, she clutched at a frail understanding that had more power than she could imagine. She realized that she would rather have an invalid in a wheelchair than not have this child at all. That night, as she let go of her fear, she was released from her lifelong struggle with the chains of worry. Her love had found its place and another small victory had been won.

Janet held her baby as they prepared to take Jordan away for surgery and would not, could not let her go. If she held her in her arms, she could protect her little love, she could delay the inevitable. It took coaxing to pry the baby out of Janet's hands so they could wheel little Jordan into the operating room. It was a six-hour surgery, but Jordan, thankfully, survived, and they managed to insert an adult cerebral shunt through which the accumulating brain fluid could drain.

Answers and miracles

Mom and Dad were now able to manage Jordan's condition, but that it had gone so far without detection tormented the doctors. The full story would not come to light until the surgeon examined the ultrasound Janet had had at 37 weeks. What he saw had him cursing. "Who missed this?!" he bellowed. The hydrocephalus was clearly evident from the scans; had they known about it, Janet would not have been permitted to go through labor. Evidently, it was the labor that had caused the baby to have a stroke and then the stroke had induced the hemorrhage. Janet eventually realized that when the baby had been stuck, the pressure would have been unbearable and the baby would have been in excruciating pain.

This next grief hit Janet on several levels. Why hadn't the problem been spotted in the ultrasound? If it had been, Jordan wouldn't have had the stroke. Her arm (now stunted and crippled) could have been normal! And how could she have allowed her baby to endure so much pain during delivery? What was life going to be like for her with all her limitations? These layers of grief would linger for a long time. They would gradually be heaped on top of a whole other series of losses and difficulties that would take years to recognize and, eventually, unpack.

And yet, in spite of their regrets, Rob and Janet could not ignore that the miracles kept coming, and they began to find hope in these mysterious events. Not only had Jordan been developing normally despite very little functioning brain tissue and no vermis, but also, when she came to after the surgery, though the nurses had said that she would not be able to nurse without vomiting, Janet had secretly begun to feed her and she had not vomited. When they checked out of the hospital,

Jordan's weight had increased by a pound, even though professionals expect that a baby will lose weight after such an operation. But the greatest marvel was that the heart of her very gruff and unemotional surgeon was melted by the astounding recovery of little Jordan. Even this crusty physician found a reason to dance, which he frequently did with Jordan in his arms as he crooned, "You are my miracle!"

Jordan entered the medical books for her extraordinary recovery, for her exceptional learning abilities, for her surprising development. She achieved some important milestones right on target. For example, Janet had been told not to worry about potty training—with the amount of brain fluid Jordan would be peeing out (the shunt drains into the abdomen where the fluid is absorbed and processed by the kidneys), it would be difficult to control her bladder—but Jordan was trained at the usual age of 2½.

In addition to all these unexpected blessings, because Janet adhered to her early decision to not worry and to empower Jordan to be everything she could be, this adorable dynamo became proficient in most of the ordinary kid activities. She played on jungle gyms, learned to ski, took dance classes, learned to ride a bike. Her life was strikingly more normal than could possibly have been imagined. Much of the despair that had been implanted in Rob and Janet's lives during these difficult years was swept away by the hope injected as a result of Jordan's amazing recovery and her remarkable accomplishments.

Tears, laughter, and beauty

But in the midst of all of these exceptional landmarks, there were also harsh realities to be faced. Janet would watch when the neighborhood children played ring-around-the-rosy. When they had to grasp each other's hands, they would deliberately avoid holding Jordan's smaller hand, her stroke hand, declaring, "That hand doesn't work." Bit by bit, the noticeable limp caused by the gradual turning in of her right foot (another result of the stroke) also became the target of relentless, malicious ridicule. Each time her head was shaved for another surgery, cruel comments and humiliation would follow her in the school yard. Each new layer of indignity set on this gentle and gracious girl would cause her mother to ache.

There would be no escaping the repeated sting of insults and scorn; her mother's heart would carry them always for her daughter. Jordan consistently, graciously would soothe, "No, it's okay, Mom. It doesn't matter. I'm okay." But Janet knew it did matter; it did hurt Jordan. It hurt them both.

Tears would come for both mother and daughter in turn. The unkindness of others was unavoidable. There was no removing the object of their ridicule, no changing the course of Jordan's life, so the pain would hit deep. But true to her character, Jordan chose to live by the creed of the surfer Bethany Hamilton, who lost her arm at the age of 13 following a shark attack: *I don't need easy, I just need possible.*

Now aged 13 herself, Jordan has been through some fifteen surgeries—five in just the last year. Multiple times, doctors have disregarded their emergency visits to the hospital with yet another tormenting headache—something Jordan describes as akin to a brain explosion—expertly declaring it to be *just another headache.* Multiple times, Janet has patiently, persistently explained to the doctors, "If you know my kid, you will know that she never complains unless it is very serious." Multiple times, she has been perceived as the nagging mother, one who is intent on her child getting more than her share of attention and squandering their time. Multiple times, she has been proven right as a shunt malfunction or other critical condition has been discovered as the cause of Jordan's excruciating pain. And again they would grieve. Grieve the time that could have been saved; grieve that the issue could have been prevented; grieve that the pain could have been avoided.

There are rare moments when this optimistic young girl dares to allow the adverse nature of her circumstances to affect her, but when it does, Janet allows Jordan's temporary perspective that "this sucks." It sucks that she has to have her head shaved again and again. It sucks that she can't make her own ponytail or button her own buttons in the mornings because of her ill-functioning arm. It sucks that she has had to patiently endure the agony of headache after headache. It sucks that she had to have another thirty stitches in her head. It sucks that she is missing grade 7 due to so much hospital time. It sucks that her hair might not grow back in time for her grade 7 leaving ceremony.

They take time to grieve these things. These issues may seem trivial in comparison to all that she has survived, but they are enormous in the heart of an adolescent. Janet gives Jordan permission to be angry, mad, sad. But only for a time: the time it takes to lament about it; the time it takes to look at the losses; the time it takes to allow the emotions to rally. When it is done, they move on so that they don't live a life of bitter regret, because as Janet says, "It will eat you alive."

She forbids their remaining in any state of remorse for too long, and as a critical strategy, to shake the heaviness of the occasional despair, they laugh. They laugh a lot. Even before surgeries, at times to the discomfort of the medical staff, they joke about what Jordan will look like; about the funny things that can happen post-surgery; about the strangeness of life ... And it works. They have a powerful sense of life being lived fully regardless of the many surgeries, the many health scares, the many painful repercussions. It has become a beautiful thing.

When you talk to Janet, there is a fascinating sense of contagious joy, but not the kind of superficial happiness that comes from a secure, well-laid-out, and neatly appointed domestic sanctuary. No, it is a gush of profound vitality that can only be achieved through adversity. It is a weighty gratitude for the gift of life, a gratitude that springs from firsthand experience of how fragile, how easily lost, life is. In young Jordan, you see a resonant grace, a peaceful maturity uncommon for someone her age. It is almost as though the physical surgeries designed to renovate her body have unexpectedly fashioned her into a luxurious and radiant soul. Jordan has, as a matter of course, become strikingly beautiful inside and out.

And the two of them have become a godsend to many other families tied to Children's Hospital. Early on, Janet recognized the shortage of supportive bodies to help families deal with the endless hours, days, months spent in the sterile monotony and with the agitating unpredictability of the hospital room. She determined to become the Welcome Wagon for any new members of what she calls *The-club-that-no-one-asked-to-be-a-part-of*. She is the self-appointed president of the club, taking it upon herself to meet a new parent with basket in hand, offering snacks, practical items (toothbrush, earplugs), a gift card for the coffee shop—anything that will help ease their stay a little and enable them to snatch a few moments of sanity in the midst of the insanity. And she weeps with families, gives them permission to feel overcome by despair as their baby, no matter how old that baby is, daily faces life and death.

It was Janet who arrived at my daughter's hospital room just days after she had recovered from her coma. It was Janet who was the first to allow me to feel the depth of despair I had been suppressing all week. It was with her, and only with her, that I felt safe enough to let my own grief begin to spill out. With just a couple of her comforting words, my tears began to flow. Few, other than those who have endured a similar grief, can understand the destabilizing, life-shaking impact on a parent when a child is diagnosed with chronic or critical illness. To talk about it—the fears, the concerns, the constant uncertainty, the strain on the family—helps to lessen the inherently overwhelming nature of hospital life.

Janet wisely reflects, "I knew that I couldn't live in the fear of the next surgery and the next surgery. I knew that if I did not learn to live one day at a time that my family would suffer." Subsequently, today they are flourishing in every way, a dynamic family with a full, rich life. A family with an incredible back story.

14

no end in sight

Rob and Janet's difficulties were not all a result of Jordan's health issues. Their continuing story is as confounding and unfathomable as it is fascinating and marvelous. For me, their expedition through loss is a survival handbook for grievers.

When Jordan was 6 months old, recovering at home from her first brain surgery, Janet discovered that she was pregnant again. The couple's initial delight was tempered by a warning from the doctor: he was not sure that the hydrocephalus was not genetic. Janet's terror was immediate. She already had one special needs baby, how could she handle two? That day, she lay on her bathroom floor screaming, unwilling to accept the prospect of another life trial.

The doctor recommended abortion as her best option. Janet had only one response to that: "You know me, doctor. Abortion is not an option for me!" She would not even tolerate the suggestion of terminating her pregnancy. She and Rob, secure in their faith, had a strong sense that God was reassuring them not to worry, that He had things under control. So with nine months to settle into it, Janet progressively looked ahead with excitement. Their new baby girl, Evie, was born healthy and strong.

With a baby and a toddler now, and still recovering from labor, Janet was carefully adjusting to incorporating the needs of a newborn with the unique medical needs of her firstborn. Then, just ten days after Evie's birth, they received a call: Rob's brother, Daniel, had been in a jet-ski accident. Janet was sleep-deprived, barely functional, but she sat near her concerned husband, offering love and support as they waited to hear more news. Within a few brief hours they were notified that things had turned for the worse; a short couple of hours later and they received the devastating report that Daniel, just 16, had died.

The family was suddenly thrown into a whole new vortex of grief. Rob's shock was extreme: he fell silent and did not speak for three days. With Rob emotionally and physically unavailable, Janet had to plow on alone with the girls, coping as best she could. One would think she had been born to cope.

And then Rob lost his job.

The move

This was now a family in acute crisis. Blindsided by shock, sorrow, and agony, both Rob and Janet had been pushed to their absolute breaking point.

When grief begins to multiply and opportunities for its release are hindered, *coping* is set in motion. Shutting down the flood of pain and escaping can be a welcome diversion. The couple decided to move to the west coast, where Janet's parents lived, to find support and start afresh in this difficult time. They were coping: Janet became Atlas, carrying her family, and the whole world, on her shoulders; Rob, still out of work, cared for the girls while Janet juggled three jobs.

But their picture of grief was not complete. In the midst of their financial pressures, Janet suddenly had a miscarriage. With too much other pain to acknowledge, this *little* loss was, by necessity, stuffed out of sight. But it did not disappear. Eventually, to their shared relief, for a few brief months, life swung to the positive side: Rob found a job; Jordan was walking and her health was stable; and the girls were daily gifts, full of life and joy. In the midst of this, Janet became pregnant once again and gave birth to a vigorous boy they named Gabe. But the grief, unaddressed, was still there, growing, covertly, agonizingly underground, undetected.

By now Janet had settled into the more domestic side of life, enjoying her new west coast neighborhood and friendships, developing a strong sense of community with close friends. But her challenges were not over yet.

A mountain of disaster

Weeks passed. One sunny spring day, Janet and Rob headed to the mountains for a day of snowboarding with a friend who was visiting from Ontario. She had chosen not to wear her helmet that day, scoffing at her husband's caution that falling on the mountain's mixture of ice, hard-pack snow, and patchy gravel would be like falling on concrete. She was undaunted, determined to enjoy the sunshine. Unlike Rob, she would not *wimp out* and wear a helmet.

A few hours later, Janet's snowboard caught an edge and she was suddenly bounced along the mountain like a ragdoll, facedown through ice and gravel. Unable to see and hysterical when Rob and the ski patrol reached her, it was obvious that her condition was critical. She was rapidly transported to the hospital. Within moments of her arrival, the trauma doctors had broken the news to Rob that Janet appeared to be brain dead. The medical staff could see her life draining away. By their assessment, she was near death.

For several hours her life teetered on the edge of the abyss, and Rob was advised to prepare for the worst. And yet, in that moment, he was strangely overwhelmed by a sense of peace that he knew was from God—God had seen them through before, He would see them through again. Astoundingly, Janet recovered. Her symptoms were those of a severe brain injury, but her CT scan inexplicably showed no bleed.

Facing the facts

Janet's main brain injury symptom was amnesia. Over the next six weeks, as she recovered in the neural critical care unit, she could not remember Rob, the children, the accident, or anything about her life. This was the beginning of a whole new series of life realities that would torment both of them. Rob would spend the morning with Janet and then sneak out for a cup of coffee. When he returned after just 15 minutes, Janet would lament, "You haven't been with me at all today! Where were you?" She was eventually forced to write everything down. It was bizarre and unnerving, and left both Rob and Janet in a state of constant uncertainty.

She had one strange, inexplicable memory of the moments when she hovered between life and death: She was with Daniel, Rob's deceased brother, but an older, adult Daniel, not the 16-year-old she had known before he passed. She recalled excitedly holding him by the shoulders and saying, "You look so good!" She remembered him urging her, "Go back, go back," but she didn't want to. And yet in an instant, she was back in the hospital, surrounded by machines, hospital staff, and her husband. Rob remains certain that this actually happened—that it wasn't a dream or Janet's imagination—because it was the only thing Janet could consistently remember throughout her period of amnesia.

The amnesia was just the start of her difficulties. Janet had to learn to write and to walk all over again. Initially she wasn't allowed to be alone with her children. And so began the real agony. She had always prided herself on being the strong one, the competent mom, the dependable friend—and now, she was just broken. Her entire identity was gone. She had no confidence in her abilities, no self-sufficiency—only feeble, endless, utter dependence. And that was where her next grief took root: she had to mourn the loss of the person she had been before the accident. From her perspective, that person had died on the mountain. She had to learn to be okay with new limitations and new methods, and she had to cry about what she could no longer do.

The letting go of our expectations of ourselves and of our lives can introduce another dimension to our grief. As Janet found, it is not only pain and limitations that need grieving, but the resulting death of plans, of aspirations, of goals, and even of life values. These need to be included on our canvas of grief. They need to be wept over and acknowledged as an equally valid loss.

Insensitive comments from well-meaning but unaware individuals can further intensify our sense of loss. Due to their never-ending traumas, Janet and Rob began to hear: "Is there something wrong with your relationship to God?"; "Are you not praying enough?" Everyone was trying to find reasons for all the *bad* circumstances this family had endured (you might secretly be thinking the same—maybe?). And sometimes Janet found herself beginning to think like them: "Well, yeah, I don't know anyone else who has had one traumatic circumstance after another like we have. Maybe we're doing something wrong ..."

It has been Janet's perspective on God and loss that I have found exceedingly liberating and hopeful. Though doubt and self-condemnation taunted her, she did not believe that God sits there and decides, "They're not praying enough, so I'm going to _____!" or "I have this lesson for them to learn, so I'll keep putting them through lots of tests." She remained steadfast in her belief that God is good and that, for whatever reasons, this was just life. Amen!

The new normal

Around 10 weeks after the accident, just when she had begun to adjust to the new normal that was life with a brain injury, Janet discovered she was pregnant again! The neural doctor warned her that a baby's cries are one of the top ten triggers for extreme mood swings, severe headaches, anxiety, and depression for brain-injured patients; that she needed to be in a dark room with no stimulation in order to continue to recover; that this might be the colicky baby she hadn't yet had; that, on all fronts, *this was not a good thing!*

But she refused to allow her injury to limit her—she was still going to live life as fully as she could—how could she do otherwise? Luckily, it was an easy pregnancy, and little Adam was born safe and healthy—a gift of a child. In utero he was quiet, patient, undemanding, and gracious, and continued to be so once out of the womb. He was a source of love, joy, and comfort for many, but most notably for Vanessa, who had just lost her precious Mattea. Adam brought cuddly warmth and love to this bereaved mom's empty arms.

The crash

Despite the joy brought by Adam, the constancy of Janet and Rob's crises were silently taking their toll. In terms of their losses, it seemed there was no end in sight. Four years after her brain injury, 7-plus years of coping with Jordan's continuous medical needs, and just months after her close friend had died of cancer, Janet finally crashed emotionally. Despite all her efforts, she could no longer function in life—everything was beginning to unravel. She was in the throes of what she now recognizes as post-traumatic stress.

Through effective counseling sessions, Janet discovered a few things. First was her lack of boundaries: having never recognized that she had limits and needs, she had to set up realistic parameters for herself. Second, Janet had always believed that she had to be good and put together—she had to let that expectation go. Third, as a people-pleaser, and never able to say "No," she had to learn the N-word. Fourth, as a hard worker who believed she could give beyond her ability, she had to learn to recognize when she was at the end of her ability. Fifth, having been taught that *anger is bad*, she had to learn to embrace and express her anger, especially as it related to her grief.

The *crash* of our grieving experiences can be a constructive time of reckoning—the perfect opportunity to *take stock* of who we are and how we function in life. Where have we neglected to acknowledge our needs, disregarded our own soul-care? On what levels have we expected ourselves and others to be perfect? In what areas have we taken on too much and not addressed our limitations? To what degree have we suppressed our true feelings preventing us from processing our grief? The answers to these questions have the potential to lift some of the added weight of everyday life from our grieving shoulders.

It took some time—years—but Janet began to change. Her internal and external beings became more effectively in sync, and she discovered real honesty. She has retained a deep compassion, but is able now to balance a positive outlook with realistic, sometimes *negative* thinking. She entrusts herself only to those who will love her for who she is and not for who they want her to be.

Processing grief

Regret lingers, though. Janet is deeply concerned for her children, for the trauma they have had to endure. Already they have seen and braved more losses than most of us will experience in a lifetime. Sometimes she has even been accused of sharing too much with her

---

kids, and must grapple with the validity (or fallacy) of this. On this level, Janet struggles with guilt, despite knowing that much of it was beyond her control.

And yet, in the name of honesty, she can't gloss over the fact that Jordan has had numerous close calls, and much pain, with her illness. They can't pretend that Janet didn't have, and doesn't still struggle with, the effects of severe brain injury. Evie's grief has shown up as a deep concern about Jordan—whenever Jordan goes into shunt malfunction, Evie fears that her sister will perish.

So Janet is careful to talk about their losses in a way that her children can understand, and to comfort them, telling them that everything is going to be all right. She's also consistent in expressing where God is in the midst of it all—she assures them that He is good. She comforts them with the knowledge that even when something bad happens, God still loves them.

As a scholar from the School of Crisis and Grief, Janet gives us her best advice:

- Encourage your friends and supporters to just listen—they'll want to make it better, but they can't.
- Don't fool yourself into believing that nothing bad will happen again—know that it can.
- Remember that you survived the last trauma—you can survive again.

Vibrant survival

In addition, Janet likes to share a vision in which she sees herself emerging from the water, as though she had been drowning. She can see that she is in a battered state—her clothes are ripped; her hair is disheveled; she is wounded, bruised, and bleeding—but notes that she is walking out on her own, no one is carrying her. She doesn't look pretty, her clothes are all torn, but she is standing and surviving.

And she is thankful. Janet rejoices that she has four phenomenal children, a healthy marriage, and an exciting and full life. I find them inspiring. Rob became the epitome of wisdom and maturity while still a young father. Janet has become the neighborhood counselor, the woman of compassion who always has time to sit down for a chat over a cup of coffee. Their four unstoppable kids who began life surrounded by so much turmoil, and who might have become sheltered by understandably protective parents, have sailed off skateboard ramps and flown off snowboard jumps, been scraped and bruised and bone-broke, but are frantically creative and profoundly happy.

I am convinced that a life lived with passion will be more full than most lives—more full of thrill, more full of disappointment, more full of joy, more full of agony. To paraphrase something Rob said Janet at the beginning of their journey:

> We have a choice: to live life in a bubble—to seal us off from the rest of the world; to put a helmet on and walk around as though we are fragile and sick—or to live and empower ourselves to be the people that we can be … You have to choose what you are going to do.

15

why me?
one family's faith questions

On a personal level, I had five years of massive losses to my name—five years of intensive education in loss. My master's was now a *fait accompli*; grieving was my specialty. My friend Carol had died from a brain tumor just months after the death of Mattea, Vanessa's baby. I had been with Carol through the night—reading to her and talking to her unconscious form while her body breathed its last murmurs of life. She died just moments after I left her bedside the next morning—she was only 41 years old. This loss represented for me the beginning of a steady stream of losses. The death of Carol, followed by my mother's death, followed by my daughter's diabetes diagnosis, piggybacked on by a whole series of spiritual miscarriages and climaxing with the sudden death of my father-in-law, all squeezed into five years, had left me crushed. I was exhausted, and was never able to get enough sleep. I had lost any will to dance, to exercise, to be active in any way. All social activity would wear me out within an hour. I became a virtual recluse, and shamed myself for being so.

Russ and I moved forward, but we were shell-shocked. Why did the crises keep coming? Why were the injustices so constant? What was going on? Had we done something wrong? Were we being taught a lesson? Why us?

When there are multiple losses, a nagging *why me?* can corrode the certainty of even the most positive of personalities. What seemed to make it harder for me was my faith background. There is a difficult negotiation with faith when the rationale behind loss has become clogged with belief systems—some that are helpful; some that really aren't.

As the daughter of a pastor, faith has always been the framework for my understanding about life and the guiding hand behind most of the life choices I have made. But faith, which is so often perceived as the means by which we can alleviate the heaviness of loss, can paradoxically cast a confusing haze over the landscape of grief, a murky swirl of doubt perpetuated by theologies and belief systems. As an example of some of the potential snares of considering loss in the light of faith, I offer up the story of Kenneth and Donna. Even if you don't come from a faith background, you might benefit from reading their story.

Donna and Kenneth had been married for many years. The constant barrage of *so-when-are-you-planning-to-have-kids?* comments kept them on the defensive about their inability to conceive. Try as they might, there was nothing they could do to change this fact. They had been trying and patiently waiting for far too long and were now quite frankly discouraged. But providence seemed to mellow when at long last, while on a European vacation one year, they discovered that Donna was finally pregnant.

The significant happening was notable, but sadly short-lived. Donna had been experiencing pain and bleeding, and by the time they arrived back in Canada, the baby had died. And yet they were hopeful. This was evidence that she could indeed conceive! With some sense of optimism, they launched into a whole battery of tests and treatments for both husband and wife to discover the source of their problems and to hopefully get pregnant again. It also set them thinking: "Everyone else is getting pregnant so easily. What's wrong with us?" Enter *shame*.

Shame

Shame presents an ego trap. Certain losses trigger questions. Others seem to be able to get pregnant, stay healthy, be successful in life. If these blessings are being given only to others, we may develop an irritating sense that something is preventing such blessings coming our way. Shame sits in that gap between a person's *expectations* and *outcomes*. There is a certain expectation around life patterns: marriage leads to babies; work leads to financial stability; friendship leads to community; vision leads to accomplishment. When, for whatever reason, expectations and outcomes do not match up, a shame zone develops.

Add to this a faith paradigm. If children are a sign of God's blessing, then lack of children logically means that blessing has been withheld. If financial prosperity indicates God's favor, then poverty means that God does not prefer me. If healing means I have faith, then continuing to be sick means I didn't have enough faith. Expectations generated from this sort of cause-effect belief can lead to shame when hopes are disappointed. Our friends were caught in the net of this trap.

In order to avoid shame, the only real options are to change the outcome (which most often is impossible) or to change our expectations. But how do you lower your expectations, or for that matter let go of them, without becoming completely apathetic or fatalistic in outlook—especially regarding major life events like pregnancy?

What Kenneth and Donna were beginning to grapple with was that so much was beyond their understanding. Expectations don't necessarily factor this in. If expectations can be replaced by expectancy, shame can be preempted. Expectations are dependent on outcomes, but expectancy is dependent on what/who I am trusting in. If I trust in a good and loving God, I can lean on His character, His kindness, His ability to bless me. For Donna and Kenneth, all they could do was wait in expectancy—God would be good to them and bless them in His time.

Two years of exhausting medical intervention were rewarded with Donna being finally pregnant again. Excited, she had an ultrasound, heard the heartbeat, and yep, there was undoubtedly a healthy baby there! Delighted, she began to settle into the idea of adding a little one to their household. Finally it was to be!

But uncertainty knocked again at their door. Spotting and cramping started to afflict the pregnant mother anew at just 14 weeks. The doctor immediately put her on bed rest. In an effort to evoke Divine intervention, a couple of close friends, people of serious faith, came over and began to pray for Donna and the baby. Miraculously, the cramping stopped. It seemed God had intervened! Relieved that the danger had passed, Donna and Kenneth rejoiced and the pregnancy continued.

This Mother's Day a sense of pleasure consumed Donna—this time next year she would be a mother, no doubt about it! However, agony was about to strike again. The cramping began again and full-blown labor kicked in. Since prayer had stopped the contractions last time, Kenneth and Donna's mom began to pray again, desperate, pleading prayers as precious minutes passed. As Donna's pain intensified, so did their prayers. They believed that the perseverance and passion of their prayers would encourage God to intervene on their behalf with another miracle. But the miraculous results were not forthcoming. And yet they kept faith: these things take time, keep going!

With greater and greater fervor they prayed. But Donna's pain was escalating, and her concern was growing. "Shouldn't we be going to the hospital?" she was silently questioning between contractions. She didn't want to stop them from praying—it would be like giving up faith in God's capacity for miracles—but she was beginning to writhe from the pain, unable to escape her dreadful torment. At this moment, Kenneth suddenly, finally, awoke from belief-induced slumber. He took one look at his wife and instantly realized she was in serious danger. They needed to call an ambulance! What was he thinking?! Couldn't he see that the prayer wasn't working?! His wife was in anguish!

The situation had turned grave by the time the paramedics finally arrived. A quick assessment determined that Donna's blood pressure had dropped too low for her to be moved. She would die if they did. But they needed to get her to a hospital as soon as possible! They had only one option: to transport her head-down. It was precarious, but their only hope. Once at the hospital, a doctor soon declared that she was out of danger. Regrettably, the baby did not survive. But Donna still had to give birth to the lifeless baby. Hope had vanished. From this day forward, all Mother's Days would be a source of deep pain for Donna.

This experience shook Kenneth's faith to its core. He had thought that they needed to show their faith by praying more, and he had almost allowed Donna to die! And why had another baby died? Where was God? They had prayed so hard! *Striving* took the stage.

Striving

Striving becomes a mind trap. Striving reasons that we must work hard in order for God to respond to our entreaties—pray harder, sacrifice more, have enough faith. It is the perception that God only responds to our efforts and our faith—that He will withhold until we measure up.

The inclination is to believe that we must prove our spiritual savvy, but if God is *Love* then is He not all about relationships? Is He not longing for us to interact with Him and include Him in the things that concern us? This proved true for Donna: shortly after her second loss, she had a vision of Jesus standing there and holding the baby in His arms. It seemed a sign of hope that He did care, that He was concerned.

In the aftermath of her second loss, Donna's doctor recommended they keep moving forward with hormone therapy. Her low progesterone levels needed to be boosted. Supplements were ordered, and in no time she was pregnant again! But the previous loss had left its mark, and she was not willing to get her hopes up. In order to protect her tiny seed of hope, she didn't let her family or friends know. She also avoided wearing maternity clothes and did all she could to keep it secret, even though they were about to move across the country to work in Montreal for a year. By the time her fifth month had come, there was a shift in her confidence; she felt it was time to celebrate that this pregnancy had now gone further than the other two.

On the day she finally dared to wear a maternity dress—Valentine's Day—her old friend *distress* paid an unexpected, unwelcome visit. Donna began spotting once more. A quick call to her new doctor in Montreal proved futile. He simply recommended that she stay off her feet and take it easy. She did as ordered, but the next day she and Kenneth faced a dilemma: weeks before, they had purchased expensive and in-demand tickets to go to a professional hockey game. Should they go? How could it hurt? She goes in, sits, and leaves? No risk there. Or so they thought.

They had not factored in the walking from the parking lot, the climbing to their seats, the stress of the crowds of people. Donna immediately sensed their mistake. By the end of the first period of game play, contractions had begun. This time Kenneth didn't wait. He swiftly rushed Donna to the hospital where she was put under overnight surveillance. By early morning, the contractions were persisting and she had dilated 2-3 cm. Concerned for the baby, the doctor went ahead and broke her waters, but suddenly the contractions ceased. She was just 23 weeks.

In the hope that she would reach 26 weeks, the time when a premature baby could survive, she was again placed on bed rest. Even so, one fear lingered—with her waters broken there was a risk of infection and this could provoke premature labor. Within just a week, infection and labor set in. Swiftly, a baby boy, David, was born. Regrettably, the infant was unable to endure the rigors of delivery and died before his tiny eyes had seen a single earthly day. Knife-like agony shot through Donna's being—physical pain that left her in absolute despair.

This time, rather than just weather the loss, Donna decided to write letters to express the anguish of losing their little boy. She knew she needed to tell the story, to recount the pain of the journey. She knew sharing would stop her from simply becoming numb and would allow her to accept the reality of this death. She had even asked for a birth certificate from the hospital so that she could have a record of his existence. But they would not give it to her. According to the medical staff, Quebec law deemed that David was not considered a baby because he had not been born alive.[69] "You just need grief counseling," they chided.

Two overwhelming emotions now enveloped her. The first was an intense fear that her tiny baby might have suffered unbearable pain— that during the trauma of delivery he would have had no one, nothing to care for him. The second was anger—she had just started to feel comfortable and peaceful about accepting the idea of the baby being okay and God had let her down. Ultimately, she was angry at God.

Sorrow suddenly became her home, bitterness her food. At the foundation of it all was the sense of betrayal. "I have believed in God, but He has betrayed me!" The tightly woven fabric of faith she had grown up with began to unravel to a tiny thread. It was all she had left, all she was holding on to. There was no Creator preserving the life of her baby, no loving Father blessing his child. God was a ruthless bandit who had stolen her boy away. *Skepticism* set in.

Skepticism

Skepticism can become a faith trap. It concludes that God can't possibly be good if an awful turn of events is allowed to happen. For Donna, if this was God, she couldn't believe in Him anymore. How could He be loving if He continued to sanction death after death when she had been honoring Him and been faithful to Him her whole life? Was it not true that God would give good gifts to those He loved? Was she therefore not loved? Would He promise a good gift and then withhold it? This was not a God to be trusted or served! In this resolution was a whole other grief—her faith was slipping out of her fingers.

In the middle of her skepticism there was a shaking off of all that she had valued with regard to faith—no more theology, no more rules, no more spiritual standards. All that she had believed and held onto her whole life had to be abandoned. From this moment on, her faith changed. She would not let go of the tiny thread she held. It was just a thread, just a fragment of the fabric of a more complex truth, but a new texture was emerging, a new dimension to the flatness of her faith. Where she could not find hope in what she knew, she began to find it in all sorts of small beauties around her—little flowers in the pavement, a tiny bird. In these basic things, she found a strange, indescribable joy. It was as though by knowing death in such an intimate way, she had become acutely aware of life. These became hope-generating in ways she couldn't express. They became her sense of God.

Religious extras disappeared, replaced by a new, simpler version of faith. A faith reduced to two essentials: God is good, and does He love me? Skepticism seems most quickly turned by unanticipated wonder. Because skepticism is linked to disappointed expectations, it can sometimes be circumvented by the marvel of an unexpected gift. This sentiment is beautifully articulated in Barbara Kingsolver's novel *The Poisonwood Bible*: "But I'll tell you a secret. When I want to take God at His word exactly, I take a peep out the window at His creation. Because that, darling, He makes fresh for us everyday, without a lot of dubious middle managers."[70]

Eventually a sense of peace swept over her, a sense that David had not known fear or pain, but instead went straight from the womb into God's arms. It was enough for now.

The year in Montreal was done, and Donna and Kenneth began the five-day trek back to the west coast by car. But before they left—surprise! Donna was 8 weeks pregnant. Since progesterone seemed to have sustained the previous pregnancy, she requested supplements from the Montreal doctors. They refused her, citing side effects. Predictably, the cramping began once more, just two days into the journey, and Kenneth immediately put her on a flight. She arrived home safely.

At 11 weeks, she finally had an ultrasound. Thrillingly, it revealed that there were two heartbeats—they had twins! Perhaps this was God's way of making up for the babies who had been lost. Twins! A new joy set in, a hopeful sense of change and blessing. But another ultrasound at 14 weeks revealed no heartbeats. These babies had also died.

This time a wrecking ball of devastation hammered them, and the torment intensified as Donna waited for her body to go into labor to deliver the two dead babies. It was more than they could endure. Their lives were now entirely shattered.

Here is where the insensitive commentators stepped in, people whose well-intentioned, but not-so-comforting observations began to harangue them. "Oh well, just try again." "At least you got pregnant—

you can get pregnant again!" "Maybe if your husband wears looser underwear...!?" Comments that were not only unhelpful but also gave no permission for grieving, so a new agony set in: *condemnation*.

Condemnation

Condemnation is poised as a soul trap. It is connected to blame. When we experience loss, especially multiple losses, we are driven to look for reasons. With childbirth, when you are a person of faith, there are only two potential objects of blame—God or yourself. If I am a good, faith-believing person, it is not appropriate to blame God— God is good, He is God. The blame therefore must be turned inward. I have done something wrong; there is something faulty in me.

For a long time, Donna was unable to move from this place of condemnation. She was locked into the sense that life was carrying on for everyone else, but she was stuck here. To make things worse, another woman in her church, one who also had struggled with her pregnancy, had stood up to testify that they had prayed, they had had *enough faith*, and their baby had lived. A cancerous disenchantment began to invade Donna. What was wrong with her? Everything pointed to the conclusion that she didn't have enough faith, that she wasn't worthy of God's blessing.

By this point the roller coaster had gone on for seven years. Every Mother's Day seemed to condemn her further. As mothers were being celebrated at church and around the city, she had only sorrow. She cried bitterly to the silent Heavenly caretaker, "Are you there? Are you good? Do you even love us?"

On the Mother's Day of that seventh year she returned from church, an acidic sorrow corroding her heart, as she burst into her lament one last time: "God, have you forgotten me?!" She languished throughout the day, hopelessness drowning her. Her heart heavy with despair and misery tight in her chest, she returned to church for the evening service. During the service, the pastor inexplicably announced:

I have a really personal word for someone. I sense God is

saying, "You asked me have I forgotten you? There are things you have endured, but you will need to endure a little longer. There are things beyond what you can see in the spirit realm, things that have to be done before the time is right."

Immediately, Donna knew this was for her. God Himself was assuring her that He cared. And she knew it not with the kind of frail, conceptual understanding of God's ways, but with a deep knowing that the God of the Universe had just touched down in that instant to meet her *personally*. It meant something. He was asking her to wait.

A full seven months later there still had been no change, and so Donna and Kenneth decided that perhaps adoption would be a good idea. They discussed taking the initial steps for adopting a child, but Donna couldn't shake the sense that God was assuring her He was about to make a way for their own baby. Courageously, she said no to pursuing adoption. Within weeks, she was pregnant. This time the doctors were vigorous with their strategies—progesterone supplements and sutures in her cervix—and it worked! A healthy baby daughter, Leslie, was born.

Body, soul, spirit

So what is the retrospective there? What had been the main problem areas? The obvious factors were her medical challenges—specifically low estrogen levels—but for Donna, the greater grief ended up connected to both her perception of faith and a lack of compassionate response from others.

With regard to their faith, like many of the believers around them, Donna and Kenneth had developed a sense that the love of God would be expressed in the *deliverance from* sorrow and pain—a spiritual anesthetic as it were. What they had discovered instead was that God would comfort them in their loss. Social scientist Brene Brown similarly articulates her experience of faith and grief in this way: "I went back to Church thinking that it would be like an epidural ... that the Church would make the pain go away ... I thought faith would say, 'I'll take away pain and discomfort,' but what it ended up saying is, 'I'll sit with you in it.'"[71]

In looking for a compassionate response, Donna herself observed that having to validate her sorrow was the hardest thing. There had been a life that had died, but no one seemed prepared to acknowledge it. Simple words might have enabled a speedier eradication of the remains of the pain; her experience could have been less tormenting had someone offered the words of comfort she so longed to hear. But where her friends had not adequately assimilated the compassion inherent in their shared faith and subsequently could not articulate comfort, she thankfully heard it instead from her God: "I'm so sorry for your loss. Can I weep awhile with you?"

Frequently faith communities as well as the North American culture in general seem to understand *sympathy* ("That's too bad"), but are short on *empathy* ("Can I weep awhile with you?"). Empathy *can't not* cry with a grieving soul. Empathy so identifies with the pain of another, that tears are unstoppable. Empathy even becomes aware of how loss impacts everyone around the situation, family members and friends because authentic relationship/community are unequivocally bound heart and soul to one another. An empathetic person dares to step down into the pit of loss, look at the landscape, and choose to lament the ruins of a life rather than attempt to do a *faith* renovation.

I add a short addition to these thoughts. In terms of the Christian faith community, the most notably absent dimension throughout the recent history of the Church—noticeable partly because it was a part of the original foundations of the faith—is dance. Barbara Ehrenreich, author and political activist, has said of Christianity and dance:

> Judging from the volume of condemnations from on high, the custom of dancing in churches was thoroughly entrenched in the late Middle Ages (1400's) and apparently tolerated—if not actually enjoyed—even by parish priests. Priests danced; women danced; whole congregations joined in. Despite the efforts of the church hierarchy, Christianity remained to a certain extent, a danced religion.[72]

There are numerous reasons why this practice was progressively outlawed by Church leadership, but its disappearance, I sense, has tragically impacted the Christian community's ability to adequately engage in everything from joy and celebration to grief. The Jewish culture has always been one of dancing, and as Jews were the first members of the Christian Church, it would stand to reason that the early Church would have embraced dance. As confirmation of this practice, throughout the history of Western cultures, dance was constantly employed as a primary activity in Church liturgies and in the celebration of Christian feast days. Conversely, dance also arose as a frequent response to the pain of grief, especially during periods of devastating loss such as the Black Plague.

I would deduce that this deficiency as connected to the Christian faith community is perhaps one of the contributing factors in the reluctance of the Church to adequately respond to a person in grief. I would suggest that an emotional disconnect between faith and practice has developed because of the inattention to the body-soul-spirit linkage—the body component has been perceptibly eradicated with the loss of dance, which had been one of the few physical manifestations of spiritual practice/worship. My conclusion? Because we don't dance anymore, our experience of spiritual community and of worship has been incomplete and on some levels impotent, rendering us ill-equipped to *flesh out* grief and give voice to deep emotion and pain. I believe we can re-establish misplaced art in faith communities and in the culture at large. We need to.

A few years ago, one of our insightful choreographers had envisioned a dance piece that gave a visual of *good grief*. In it, individuals (the *grievers*) are being controlled and carried by other dancers—it was a sense of one being gripped by fear, pain, or some other oppressive force. Throughout the piece the victims are being pushed and prodded and pulled without any sense of their own ability to control the outcome. Into the picture come two dancers who approach those in distress, chasing away their oppressors with a calm, caring authority, and then begin to dance slowly, peacefully—as though the body is beginning to exert itself after debilitating pain. The grievers begin to mimic the dance, gaining more and more liberty in their physical selves.

More dancers enter, and now the movement, echoed by many, begins to evoke a soothing sense of support, encouragement, community, hope. In a moment the movement picks up speed and all the dancers have suddenly removed the colorful fabrics that have been tied around their waists. Now flashes of color ripple through the scene with every gesture of the arms, the unison flutter of the fabrics giving the impression that yet another group of colorful dancers has magically entered the space. The movement escalates—limbs, bodies and colors whirling and flowing with increasing freedom and irresistible beauty—and reaches for its climax. The fabrics are suddenly launched, sailing into the air like dancers floating to the heavens with a declaration of final release.

Loss. Pain. Community. Care. Shedding grief. Peace.

16

remains of the pain

*a*n American doctor was visiting a community in Angola on one of his frequent medical visits to this African nation. On this particular day, a woman had come to him and, through an interpreter, had communicated her desperation: "Can you please help me? I have been pregnant for eight years." Presuming that there had been a mistranslation (eight years?) and seeing that the woman didn't really look pregnant, he said a few pseudo-comforting comments and then excused himself to his more urgent work.

The following year, the doctor was back in the same community and the same woman came to him with a similar complaint: "Can you please help me? I have been pregnant for nine years." He was suddenly alert. "Nine years," she had said. Looking at the woman with a more perceptive eye, he puzzled afresh. How was this possible? She looked reasonably normal, but he decided to go ahead with an internal examination. To his great shock and utter distress, he discovered that the woman was indeed pregnant and had been so these last nine years. The evidence was in the calcified corpse of a tiny baby still in her womb. The embryonic infant had died those many years ago but the body had not been expelled. The doctor immediately set to work to remove the rigid mass from its mother's uterus and the relieved woman went on her way.

It would be another year before the doctor next encountered the formerly ailing woman. This time she came to him glowing with the smile of one who has been freed. As he came close, he was amazed and delighted to see that her physical form had changed again: her belly bulged, bearing witness to the fact that she was finally, after ten long years, pregnant with a new life.

Our ungrieved losses literally become the unbirthed fetuses that prevent the conception of new dreams and fresh expectancy for the future. If we are ever to dare to dream again, our beings need to expel the persisting remnants of past deaths and purge our hearts in order to conceive hope again.

For our own reference, it might also be helpful to do a quick assessment of what might be considered a stuck grieving process. Grief counselor Glynis Sherwood compiled a list of the symptoms of incomplete grieving:[73]

- The pain of loss intensifies or feelings of numbness don't abate, at least 6 months to 1 year after the loss.
- Preoccupation with the loss. Intense longing for a lost loved one or former life.
- Bitterness and/or rage.
- Difficulty acknowledging the loss has occurred. Repressing thoughts about the loss. Avoiding situations that are reminders of the loss.
- Depression—especially hopeless thoughts and feelings.
- Apathy sets in—aka giving up because I just don't care.
- Relationship strain—problems with intimacy, or withdrawing from friends and social activities.
- Experiencing distressing, intrusive thoughts related to the loss.
- Believing life no longer has meaning or purpose.
- Increased irritability or agitation.

There is a strange sticky-ness to grief. It has an aggravating habit of lingering well beyond the months, years that seem appropriate for its impact. Its unhappy influence seems intent on coloring much of the aftermath of loss with an obscured view through the window of the future. It is difficult to believe in good things when losses have been especially painful or numerous. The ability to conceive hope for the future is constantly thwarted by the remembrance, the ache, the residual regrets of loss. Fear, unforgiveness, trauma, and victimization can inhibit the conception of new dreams and expectancy for good things to come.

Removing fear

Fear is a frequent by-product that can secretly delay recovery from mourning. There is a natural response mechanism in fear that is designed to caution us against further pain and loss. Unfortunately, this protective mechanism can itself become detrimental, as Dr. Paul Brand has observed: "When people are in pain, when the pain evokes fear, then the pain gets worse. If the fear can be allayed ... the pain diminishes."[74] Facing our fear and dismantling it seems critical in order to restore us after loss.

Recall our young friend Jordan, who had braved so many operations and recoveries. But there was one surgery that left her in a chronic state of fear. This surgery was on the tendons of her leg to repair its twisting. The surgery resulted in excruciating pain whenever her leg moved or twitched even slightly. The doctor had warned that "Even adults find this pain unbearable!" The aftermath of the trauma from this operation was that every subsequent surgery would evoke an immediate and severe reaction from the girl: "No, no, Mom. I can't do this!" Her tears would flow unchecked and her terror would be acute. It has taken several counseling sessions for Jordan to be able to face the prospect of any surgery with courage again, but she has been overcoming her fear.

Conversely, an overall resistance to fear can have surprising results. My friend Mike called me a number of years back. He was writing his autobiography and had come upon the subject of the chronic illness Parkinson's disease, which had overtaken his physical health in recent years. Many people had puzzled over his consistently buoyant outlook. He showed no signs of the emotional pain that would have been expected with such a debilitating illness. He was calling me because he knew I read the Bible. He wanted to know if I recalled the *Charlie Brown Christmas* cartoon where Linus quotes a passage about the birth of Jesus: "You know where the shepherds see a whole crowd of angels and Linus says, 'and they were sore afraid?' Does it really say 'sore' s-o-r-e?" After looking it up in the old King James version, I called him back to affirm, that, yes, it was s-o-r-e. What was his premise? He sensed that pain was connected to fear (that is, the shepherds were sore because they were afraid) and believed that he was not experiencing any significant emotional pain connected to his illness because he was not afraid. A good thought.

Releasing forgiveness

I noted in an earlier chapter that forgiveness is an important component in freeing ourselves from the bitterness that can follow grief. Presumably, therefore, unforgiveness can be another inhibitor to our conception of new dreams for the future. There is no denying that when unjust circumstances surround our experiences of grief and when there is no apology or indication of restitution, it seems we have a right to withhold our forgiveness.

Aleena is a gorgeous and gentle woman who was in her late twenties when she married Andrew. They had spent a good 15 months getting to know one another before taking the plunge into marriage. She had made the appropriate assessment of their suitability—a common outlook on life, faith, and career direction, and above all, they loved one another deeply. She had confidently determined that marriage was the next logical step.

But something insidious had been lingering in the background. Just six months after their lovely outdoor wedding, friends and family witnessing their declaration of lifelong fidelity to one another, Aleena discovered a sickening truth. Andrew had been living a double life. Aleena had discovered that her beloved had been harboring a sexual addiction—secretly contacting women online, under another identity, to engage in no-strings-attached sexual affairs. It had been going on since well before they were married, but she had not allowed herself to see it. She had ignored the cues in their dating relationship: the lack of authenticity, the immaturity, the self-righteousness, and defensiveness when his behavior was questioned. She had chosen, instead, to believe the best about him, but in doing so, she had ignored her own intuition.

Although he had been nominally repentant and apologetic when she confronted him with his infidelity, after just a few weeks of counseling it was evident that his cycle of denial and lies was ongoing. All of this was further aggravated and defended by his family, who justified his behavior, regarding Aleena as the one who had deceived. In a matter of months, his confession turned to accusation, with Andrew now claiming that the people who were walking them through this crisis were controlling Aleena and pitting her against him. Self-deception had begun to take root as he launched into belittling and berating his wife with a profusion of manipulative words that tormented and confused her. There was little left of her sane self when he finally moved to another city, divorcing her and leaving her alone in a heap of rejection, abandonment, and unpardonable heartache.

How does a person proceed with life when the perpetrator of their pain disappears from the scene, is unapologetic, refuses to acknowledge his or her wrongdoing? The most common, possibly the most acceptable, response is unforgiveness. It seems right, doesn't it? They don't deserve our forgiveness.

But we saw it with the Rwandan widows: there is no freedom for the victim if they do not forgive. Unforgiveness eats at us, it erodes our joy, it plunders our peace, it blocks our personal growth. Forgiveness is an invaluable response that ultimately frees our souls from the hurtful actions, the damaging incidents, the painful results of the past.

Recognizing her need to move forward with life, Aleena faced a painful reality: she needed to forgive Andrew. She would need to trust a Heavenly Judge to vindicate her, but she was not going to truly live unless she released him and this calcified remnant of a marriage. Through months of counseling, she was able to understand Andrew's brokenness and addiction, his self-deception and the justification of his behavior as enabled by his immediate family. She forgave Andrew for betraying their covenant of marriage and for abandoning her.

Aleena has just married again. Jason, her new husband, is joyful and gracious, and possesses a generous spirit. For Aleena, it is brand new beginning. The pain of the past is gone, albeit not forgotten.

Dislodging trauma

Many of the events I have recounted in this book resulted in un-imaginable trauma for those who experienced them. Regrettably, trauma can also prevent the expulsion of the losses of the past. The dictionary definition of trauma is "emotional shock following a stressful event or a physical injury, which may be associated with physical shock and sometimes leads to long-term neurosis."[76]

I am remembering a trauma in my strong of losses that I have nev-er acknowledged. My teenaged daughter found my father-in-law, Norm, dead on the floor of our living room. She had called to me and I came running. The shop vac was blaring as he lay on the floor beside it—he had been refinishing our floors in preparation for our move that month, using the vacuum to suck up the sawdust. Norm was gray and motionless. I knew in an instant he was gone, but I nonetheless called 911. The operator led me through the necessary steps for CPR, which I recited to my daughter, who responded obe-diently. His delicate ribs bent and squeezed as she pressed with full force on his chest; she felt them crack. His lungs huffed and grunt-ed, but there was no breath coming. It was an eternity before the paramedics arrived; I had taken my turn with compressions, but I knew it was all pointless.

Norman had defied death multiple times. His heart, his big, caring, compassionate heart, had developed an infection after he fell from a ladder, and he lived with a replacement valve in it. Consequen-tial medical issues had been numerous, and my mother-in-law had, more than once, been thrown into an emotional tizzy as yet another calamity threatened the mortality of her husband. But he kept go-ing, like the 30-year-old ladder that had caused his fall. "I have never had problems with that ladder for more than 30 years. I can't un-derstand why it should have broken now," he had reasoned. As with his health, he had not adequately factored in age and deterioration.

And so he had crawled around on the floor that day, sanding and varnishing our floors until his heart gave up and laid him out in a sideways heap on the hardwood, the vacuum still blaring. I had gone into what my mom always called her *supervisor mode* and had done what needed to be done. My mom, a nurse, was the night supervisor of her hospital, and in supervisor mode, her emotions would be shut down and even the most traumatic circumstances would be handled matter-of-factly so she could take control of the situation.

I don't think I had allowed myself to acknowledge my inconvenient emotions about Norm's death. Not for lack of wanting to, but because my inner supervisor was preoccupied by so many practical things in those weeks. There was now a funeral to be planned, and the week of the funeral we still had to move—a whole household and studio needed to be packed up and moved into storage, with no prospect of a new home/location on the horizon. Our roof had been leaking, and there was torrential rain on the day we moved. The water was pouring down the tarps Russ had tacked up in the laundry room to funnel it into large garbage buckets. The volume and density had been too much for the tarps, and now the rain was pouring in everywhere. Our landlord had been furious, blaming us and berating us all the way out the door.

In addition to all of that, during the funeral weekend, a business associate with whom I had been in contract for a new studio development in Vancouver had called to announce that she had given the whole program over to another person. I had already put out all our promotional material and had invested a full year in that new project. And then a business associate of Russ had contacted him to let him know that the tens of thousands of dollars that were owing from a massive arts initiative were our responsibility. But we had no financial resources to draw from.

We were numb throughout that summer. Our family of five had moved in with Russ's mom to support her after Norm's death, but we couldn't acknowledge the depth of our losses. We had to just cope. It was not until September, when we moved into our own home, that the emotional anesthetic finally wore off and we began to feel the pain. And not just a little pain, but the cumulative pain from the five years of losses we had been through.

We hunkered down in our new home, spent lots of time together as a family, bought a puppy, and began to process the pain. Intuitively, we knew that there would be no moving forward with life until we did some soul care. It was a lonely year. Many of our friends seemed bothered by our *negativity*—that heaviness that comes from grief—and stopped calling us or hanging out with us. Our presence at parties and social events seemed inconvenient, awkward, so we stayed a home a lot.

But loneliness became our truest friend. Loneliness gave us permission to release our tears, vent our anger, cast our blame, and wade through much unresolved history. We lingered for a long time in depression and hopelessness, and loneliness did not judge us or try to coerce us into accepting a plastic replica of hope. We sensed genuine hope would be given birth to once our emotional wombs were cleared. Hope has been appearing on the horizon, a slow dawning of sunrise. And we have been recovering ... gradually.

As a beginning to this new season, Russ and I decided to begin to dance together. For the first time ever, we took dance classes as a couple. Swing dancing was our choice. It was a new form of dance for me, but it provided a levity that proved to be just what we needed at that time. Where the contemporary dance I was primarily trained in might have contributed to the deeper emotions that needed expressing, it would have been too intense, perhaps too painful at that stage. Swing brought joy, fun, and endorphins, and prevented me from becoming critical of my dancing technique after months of not dancing.

Resisting victimization

If I am to be honest, there are times when loss becomes just too much (too many losses, too many injustices), leaving the heart in a hazy cloud of *victimization*, a blurry fog that obscures the horizon of hope. "This always happens to me!" is the battle cry of a victim. True, I may be one of those for whom the losses have inexplicably been more frequent, but the *always* is an indicator of something more. *Always* seems to suggest an inability to break free from a pattern of loss. It reveals a perception that my experiences are worse than those of others; that my hands are tied and I'm not capable of changing the course of my life. Not true.

Victimization can lock us into not only a mindset of hopelessness, but also behaviors that can produce more loss in the future. If my losses have been about rejection, my sense of being victimized by others' rejection will unwittingly create behaviors that cause people to feel awkward or unable to connect with me ... which of course looks like more rejection. If I make a general assessment of life from the perception that because it happened before, it will keep happening, I will see it occurring again and again, even when it's not. If there is a sense that some cosmic power has a vendetta against me, I can develop a pseudo-superstitious or overly cautious interaction with life: "I have to be careful that I don't _____ or else _____," or "I don't dare trying new things because something always goes wrong."

These declarations and perceptions can keep us locked into a belief system and an evaluation of life that becomes self-fulfilling prophecy. My losses didn't happen because I didn't believe right—losses just happen. Victimization is about staying in a place where life events and circumstances are constantly assessed through the lens of perpetual powerlessness. Restoring power or empowering myself becomes a matter of embracing the courage to take a single next step in the direction of hope so that, step-by-step, new dreams and new vision are again conceived.

I need to tell you a little bit more about my father. Tom Oshiro has always been a man of irresistible charisma. Whether we run into high school buddies who played with him on the football team more than 68 years ago, or meet up with mayors of towns he has been a pastor in, or chat with the street people he has cared for these last twenty-odd years, the response is always the same: "Your dad is such a kind and generous man! We love him and we know we are loved by him!"

In response to the losses of the past, my dad chose to overcome by reversing the focus. When his Japanese looks were the source of isolation, he focused on his athleticism, people skills, and compelling leadership, causing people to become racially blind—among other things, he became a top quarterback, the president of his student council, and citizen of the year. Where his past was about poverty and hardship, he is generous to a fault—there is not a person who comes to him in financial need whom he won't give money to, even when his own finances are sparse. Where his history was about his being treated as an enemy alien, he has chosen to love and embrace even the most rejected people of the communities around him—from drug addicts to the poor, to criminals, to those struggling with mental illness.

My dad has been an inspiration to everyone around him, and it has been predominantly due to the fact that he chose not to position himself as a victim. He has courageously chosen, instead, to persevere with an attitude of *my-life-and-my-character-are-being-transformed-by-these-experiences* and this, curiously, has cleared the internal fog so that his hope has been restored.

I am aware that, in the same way pain can come as severed nerves begin to regenerate, there can be an acute pain when our numbed selves begin to acknowledge the loss(es) we have experienced. Victimization can grow from these feelings ("Why does everything *always* have to hurt me so much?!")—and it is a temptation to numb once again—but a change in mindset can alter the perception of this pain. When I go to my massage therapist for treatment, there is most often pain that comes with a massage, but knowing that the pain will improve my a knotted muscles, I can force my being to interpret this as a *good* pain so that I can endure it. So too will an acknowledgement of *the good pain that grieving is* enable the soul to accept the temporary agony that comes with submitting ourselves to its therapy rather than feeling like a victim.

Accepting suffering

There is one final perspective that seems akin to my last thought and that I sense can liberate us from being stuck in grief, and that is to *accept suffering*. Again, you will need to stay with me on this one since it is not quite what it seems. As mentioned earlier, with the dawn of anesthetics, epidurals, and pain-relieving medications, we became a culture that believed even the most minor of our pains could be inhibited. We essentially became a generation that sought to annihilate suffering. Unfortunately, we also paired it with the belief that suffering is therefore wrong. But is it?

What if we believed that suffering is not wrong? What if we believed that suffering is just part of life?

This realization came to my friend Sandy when she was in the midst of cancer treatments. Sandy's candid documentation of her journey unexpectedly exhumed hope at a time of unthinkable suffering. Her sometimes hilarious insights into the absurdity of life with a terminal illness—especially one inflicted on a person's most personal and intimate bodily regions—are a surprisingly welcome study in paradoxes. The following excerpt from her blog is not only compelling, but also acutely soul-challenging.

Yesterday afternoon as I sat in the sun, I had an epiphany.

Since my cancer was first diagnosed on August 31, I've been able to see the power, and beauty, and truth of my experiences throughout this long and arduous journey: the flashes of incandescence I wrote about a couple of weeks ago. Sickness, suffering, anxiety and fear have new faces, new sweetness that I was never able to see until they became the constant companions of my nights. I knew that my suffering was achieving for me a new perspective, a more refined character, a deeper joy. And I even described this year as a gift. But what I didn't realize until yesterday is that it's not the year that's the gift. It's the cancer. The cancer is the bag of gold dropped into my lap to enrich my life.

It's almost as if those dreams I had last week brought the last of my dread to the surface to dissipate in the light of day, freeing me to embrace the rest of my treatment rather than flinching from it; and teaching me to feel enriched by the cancer rather than robbed by it.

I'm still reeling with the wonder of it all.

And it might not make sense to anyone but me.

And it might be the deranged ponderings of a chemo fried brain.

But it might be the truth. And it might help me make it through the last few weeks of my treatments, because now I think I might be able to walk up the stairs of the hospital without a clenching dread gnawing at my heart. And on the days when I am away from myself, I might be able to rest instead of fight. I might be able to surrender myself to the befuddlement rather than struggle for clarity and control. Maybe this is the last front in my war for control. Maybe this is where I finally lay down my arms and sign for peace. Or maybe it's just another skirmish.[77]

My dear Sandy lost her battle with cancer in 2010, but not before gifting us with volumes of her profound thoughts and reflections on God, faith, healing, and pain.

I don't want to undermine or dismiss the deep agony that many are experiencing at this very moment; my comments are in no way an attempt to implant guilt or put pressure on those grappling for peace through pain. My friend's insights were the result of a long and onerous process, an embracing of suffering and a walking through the valley of the shadow of death. Sandy was a woman honestly confronting her fears and her struggles. These are discoveries borne out of revelation, not determination. And what was at the core of that revelation? There was no need for her to exert control, no need for the frail and crumbling edifice of expectations. She needed only to resign herself to the expectancy that someone with a greater understanding of her need was in control. As she says, it was all giving her "a new perspective, a more refined character, a deeper joy." Some describe it as finding peace, and it is here that hope can be conceived again.

Sandy's daughter, Anna, and one of Sandy's closest family friends, Sarah, danced at her funeral. Sarah had asked to be able to dance when they informed the students at her school (also the place where Sandy taught), but she had been told that it was inappropriate, not what was needed in that moment. Sarah, just 17, could only see one way to process her paralyzing pain—she had to let it out physically. She had to dance!

The funeral organizers understood. They understood that the deep

love for and emotional connection to this beloved friend, this trea-
sured mother, needed more than just words to express the loss.
Dance would release this grief, help those left behind to find peace,
to be able to hope again. And so Sarah and Anna danced out the
remains of the pain.

17

dancing to dream again

Oh, the mystery of how hope is finally conceived and a person can venture to dream again. The rebirth of hope follows no pattern or schedule. Just as the physical healing process of our bodies is a miraculous one, so too is the healing of the soul. Here I circle back to my friend Vanessa.

In the years that followed the death of Mattea, Vanessa was a model of vulnerability and courage. I have marveled as she dared to believe for new births, even though her initial loss was so staggering. A year or so after Mattea's death, Vanessa gave birth to a gorgeous little boy whom she named Jonah.

Complications with the enormous fibroid that had hindered Mattea's safe birth also jeopardized Vanessa's pregnancy with Jonah. The threat of a second loss plagued her as the softball-sized fibroid, bolstered by pregnancy hormones, continued to grow as the baby grew, the two competing for space. But Jonah was born safely, sneaking into the world at the moment the medical personnel, thinking he was in danger, were scrambling to prepare for an emergency intervention. Their backs were turned when he arrived.

And then just two years later, Vanessa was pregnant again. She gave birth to another boy, this one named Tobe. As she approached the last days of her pregnancy with Tobe, something began to concern the doctors. It seemed the baby was not turning in preparation for delivery and the professionals determined that they were going to need to execute a complex maneuver to turn him. Again, the fibroid was complicating what could have been a relatively simple procedure. Vanessa was naturally alarmed and anxious. Fortunately, the day before the medical intervention was scheduled, Vanessa's midwife had encouraged her to go see a woman who was skilled in understanding the emotional connection between mother and baby in hopes that there might be an alternative to the medical intervention.

Vanessa sat with the woman, who began to ask questions about her history—life, children, and births—and made an immediate discovery. Although Vanessa was pleased to be pregnant again, she had secretly hoped that this new baby would be a girl. Disappointed that she was having another boy, she was afraid that she would not be able to connect with a son instead of the desired-for daughter. The woman led Vanessa in an exercise in which my distressed friend began to speak words of love and affirmation to the baby in her womb. She declared (through tears from her lingering disappointment and fear) that she was excited for him to be born, that he was precious to her—that she was glad he was a boy.

Call it coincidence—the doctors certainly did—but the next morning, when Vanessa arrived at the hospital to have the baby turned, a quick examination by the medical staff showed, to their great astonishment, that the baby had taken matters into his own hands, as it were. Vanessa's immediate thought was: Could it be possible that those words of love, and a renunciation of the fear, had the ability to produce a physical change for the baby in utero? She believes so.

A new pregnancy, an apology, a new opportunity can be fresh emotional canvases on which to re-imagine possibilities, and are necessary to move back into living life fully. Although the resolution of loss is not always neatly tied up—life is neither a novel nor a Hollywood movie—even small infusions of altered perspective can re-establish the soul's equilibrium.

Restoration

For me, small gifts of kindness and compassion have been life-giving. My childhood friends, those who had rejected me in junior high, accepted me back into their group after a year of exclusion and continued to be my closest friends throughout high school. Funny, though, for some thirty-odd years, none of them ever acknowledged that year of rejection. I had already forgiven them and had worked through my emotional hurts, though, so all was good.

But as we all were heading into our late forties, one friend finally came to me after a reunion dinner and said, "You know, I don't think I've ever said sorry for what we did to you back then. It was unkind, I'm so sorry." I can't explain how deeply it touched me that she would care to offer such a kindness those many years later. Another friend had an epiphany when a niece of hers was going through a rejection experience very similar to mine. She suddenly realized, "This is exactly what we did to Sandy!" She came to me in person with a heartfelt apology—a grown woman saying sorry for an adolescent blunder. The 12-year-old in me was deeply impacted.

A word of identification and compassion can provide water for the soul, but an apology releases a flood of healing.

In 1988, the Canadian government eventually apologized for the experience of my father's family (and others like them) during World War II, with an initiative called the Japanese Redress.[78] Every Japanese Canadian who was affected by the internment and the restrictions imposed by the government was given $21,000 as compensation for what was lost. It didn't completely restore the $443 million that was taken from the population of Japanese Canadians, but it was a significant act by a national government. For us, that Christmas was hysterical. Unaware of the sudden financial infusion, my siblings and I grew concerned when my typically generous, but financially strapped, father began pulling out another and then another and then another gift, multiple gifts for each of us. We were looking at one another, thinking, "This man has blown a gasket! What's up?" When he then placed a check for $1,000 in each of our laps, we were convinced that he had indeed lost it. He let us know of the redress after he had gleefully shocked us all with a bounty of presents.

Gratitude and giving

I am grateful that some of my losses have been countered by reconciliation and restoration, but what about the times when this is not the case? Sometimes babies hoped for are never conceived, sometimes apologies don't come, and sometimes new opportunities don't present themselves. What then?

It might sound simplistic in terms of strategies, but *gratitude* can help soothe a devastated psyche. Thankfulness reclaims the beauty in a life. Those wonderful Rwandan widows will forever be my inspiration on this front. After we led them through their process of grieving, I asked them, "So, do you regret that you have had to live through all of this [the genocide]?" Overwhelmingly, the response was, "No, I am thankful I am still living and since I'm alive, there must be a purpose for me."

I'm so pathetically inclined to feel sorry for myself. To lament all the difficulties I've had to endure. But once the grieving is done and I have lamented for the time that I need to, gratitude and thankfulness can help to strip off my mourning clothes, my black. Like Vanessa, who became grateful for the lap of the ocean waves, or Donna, who appreciated the beauty of a tiny flower, simple thankfulness can begin to generate a new perception of reality. And all it needs is small things: I ate today; I have a husband who loves me; the sun was shining; the mountains outside my window are stunning; I have a home, a bed, friends.

The darker the night, the brighter the stars. (Dostoyevsky)[79]

Grief, strangely, can become the blessing of contrasts. Truly, in coming out of a storm, the normal can feel calmer. In coming out of a cave, the day can appear brighter. In coming out of numbness, the senses can be more awakened. Like a blind man seeing for the first time, grief can make the ordinary seem extraordinary. And this, quite naturally, can provoke the very thankfulness that can bring restoration.

In my international travel I have frequently seen that the people who have experienced the most devastation, and those who possess the least, often have the most thankfulness, express the most gratitude, the most appreciation. Having little can induce thankfulness for the slightest blessing. We once visited a woman who lived in an alley in the streets of Manila. There, between the walls of two large brick buildings, in a space of six feet by six feet, she had set up her home, one made of two-by-fours and plywood on a dirt floor. She had even created a second floor, where she and her seven children slept.

This was not an embittered woman who gave up hope when her husband left her for another woman. This was not a forlorn mother who pitied herself for having to provide for her seven children. This was not an unfortunate individual from a developing nation who felt ashamed of how little she had in the presence of someone from a first world nation. No, this was a woman whose thankfulness went so deep that when I pointed out the lovely paper fan she had mounted on her wall (it was the only ornamentation in the whole place and I had desperately been looking for something to compliment her on in the shock of seeing how and where she lived), she completely confounded me by gifting that fan to me the following day.

Thankfulness does not replace what has been lost or smooth the ripple of the impact of loss. But it does revive me, and it encourages me to look outward after a long, grievous period of reflecting inward. I am finding that grief has sensitized me to others and their pain, and has increased my capacity for care and compassion. Foundationally, grief has increased my desire to give what I can to help others, and that generates more life, more hope, and sheds all that hopelessness.

Ultimately, I see something reassuringly beautiful as I understand more and more that loss does not need to be feared. I see a tree at its climax of beauty, the stunning reds and golds and bronzes of the fall, the time just before its yearly death when it is still glorious. It's a promise from Jeremiah:

> Their lives will be like a well-watered garden,
> never again left to dry up.

> Young women will dance and be happy,
> young men and old men will join in.
> I'll convert their weeping into laughter,
> lavishing comfort, invading their grief with joy.
> Ending with new beginnings.[80]

Vanessa and I have become comrades in grief. The ebb and flow of loss—the carrying and leaning and weeping and despairing and re-pairing—have created a robust alloy from our two inseparably affixed hearts. Vanessa is pregnant again. The fibroid has been removed, and she is daring to risk another pregnancy. No telling if this will finally be her little girl, but at this point, it doesn't really matter. Her two amazing little boys have won everyone's hearts, especially their mama's, and she knows that joy can come even when life goes differently than expected.

I am daring to risk again too—I'm pregnant with a new sense of the future. I have built another studio and am investing in a whole new crowd of friendships, a collection of young women to mentor, and have a new vision for what might be ahead. I have twinges of fear, of course. At times I fear that past losses will repeat themselves—and maybe they will. But as I coach myself through this new pregnancy of expectancies, I see a whole other beautiful dimension emerging.

Vanessa and I have been learning to dance with "a broken heart that doesn't seal back up" as Anne Lamott says. At times our pain keeps us awkwardly caring for one another—sometimes the stiff-armed angry phases of our grief push others away. But even this is a dance—a partner work in which one is drawn in close and then spun out alone into the expanse of the dance floor, but never too far to be run to, lifted, carried, cared for. Again, Anne Lamott articulates it well: "And you come through, and you learn to dance with a banged up heart. You dance to the absurdities of life; you dance to the minuet of old friendships."[81]

The dancers who have journeyed with us these few years have all been scarred by grief, and many of their stories are here. You might think we'd be a sad crowd. We're not. As a matter of fact, we laugh together more than is normal. I often go to bed with a whole crowd of dancers still in my family room, laughter dancing up the stairwell as I attempt to fall asleep. Perhaps it's that contrast idea again: with the season of grief being so heavy, other parts of life seem so much lighter.

And together we are creating a dance production connected to this book. We are taking stories of grief and recovery from loss and pouring them through the creative sensibilities of our group of talented dancers. All the words that can't be written here will find their voice in the movements of the dancers. Maybe you will watch it one day, but for now let our stories dance in you.

encore: pausing for grief

Grief is inevitable. We live. We love. We grieve. We move on. Of course, none of this is so simple, straightforward, or swift. So how do we begin to process our grief if we have not yet begun? And how do we know when there is still grieving to be done? There are times when our body will begin to tell us, to show outward signs that we need to slow down to address the emotional parasite that has hijacked our physical well-being. It is as the writer C.S. Lewis said: "And no one ever told me about the laziness of grief."[72]

How do we contend with this plunderer of our faculties? Most of us in the Western world soldier on. We typically resist every physical cue that runs through the streets of our bodies like some lone town crier, declaring our emotional curfew and decreeing that it is time to close up shop, lower the lamps of activity, and settle in for a night of quiet. We don't like its demands—after all, are we not the most important performers on the stage that is our lives? There are no understudies for this drama ...

If we dare to listen, he will cry it again: "Stop! It's time to discontinue all this activity and *be*." Fighting against this internal resistance is like persistently shoving against a rusted gear—it does no good, it will not improve the movement, it may even cause the whole thing to seize. Slowing down, resting, restoring, lubricates the gears, and renders the body functional in due time.

The key to recovery, really, is to prod the parasympathetic nervous system into operation. How do we do that? Paradoxically, we STOP.

STOP and ...

I am reluctant to make this into a *self-help* book, but as I experienced, sometimes we almost need *permission* to care for ourselves and focus on our real needs. And so, here is a beginner's guide to learning to STOP.

---

1. STOP and Listen

- Your body and emotions are speaking to you: listen to what they are saying about your current situation and circumstances.

- You will be able to detect any *negative* symptoms that might indicate that something (in your emotions, in your perspective, in your body) needs your attention.

- Let those who are close to you know what you need, and encourage them to give you permission to remain in this season of grief for as long as you need to.

2. STOP and Breathe

- Learn to take deep, cleansing breaths. Breathing helps to trigger your parasympathetic nervous system. And you can do it wherever you are, no equipment required.

3. STOP and Rest

- Find a time and a place where there is zero demand on you.

- Pause to put your feet up, do nothing, momentarily let go of anything and everything that might disturb you. This mostly means that all electronic devices should be turned off: anything that buzzes, beeps, rings, or keeps you on guard. You might need to let people know that you do that every once in awhile.

4. STOP and Eat

- Keep putting healthy food in your mouth. Healthy food, well digested, fuels your cells and staves off illness.

- Resist eating on the run, if you can, and make meals that matter.

- A meal eaten while you're still nursing the stresses of the day can exacerbate any existing digestive problems. Remember that when the sympathetic nervous system has been activated by stress, it diverts blood away from the digestive system so that it does not function at its normal capacity.

- Budget time each day to make a healthy meal (or make them all on a single day and freeze some). If you have trouble justifying the amount of time it takes to make a healthy meal, especially when your days are busy, consider how many more days/hours are lost because of ill health.
- Ask for help: people don't always know what to do for you when you are grieving, so you can perhaps request they bring meals.

5. STOP and Be

- Be present in life, as raw and as real as you need to be, and embrace what is happening *now*. It will possibly mean slowing down as your responses to life will be slower than normal, but let yourself sit back and truly experience your life.
- *Doing* can be your greatest enemy. Remember that you are a human *being* not a human *doing*.

6. STOP and Weep

- The tears are there more often than we dare to acknowledge. Pulling away to just let them come is revitalizing. There is no need to analyze why or what it is about; just let your soul vent through your tear ducts.

7. STOP and Enjoy

- Appreciate life and respond in gratitude for it.
- Begin to make note of the small blessings of life: family, sunshine, laughter, love, shelter, health, freedom.

8. STOP Should-ing on Yourself

- Resist the temptation to make the above a list of everything you *should* be doing.

- *Do* and *be* only what you truly can. You are just one person—and by the way, you're not superhuman.

- Remove all expectations and be realistic about what you can actually accomplish right now and what you can't; be prepared to adjust your plans and projects accordingly.

- Let others deal with their expectations of you. Sure, you will more than likely let someone down, but IT WON'T BE THE END OF THE WORLD.

- If you are a people-pleaser, and you've always believed the lie that people only like you when you are fun to be with and put together, here is where your *true friends* get to show you their unconditional love for who you really are. Not only that, but you get to be in the position of receiving. It may be hard, but you need to let others be the givers. (Look at it as giving them the gift of giving, if that makes you feel better.)

- Remember what Anne Lamott said: "*No* is a complete sentence."[83]

9. STOP and Dance

- You may have never considered yourself a dancer, but you more than likely danced when you were a child; you may not think you even know how to dance, but you knew what to do before you became self-conscious and aware of how others perceive you. I would suggest that your body and your emotions would like you to go back to those days of inner freedom.

- Call it your "Shaking Off Grief" dance and literally do that: shake your limbs free of the heaviness of loss. You may find it surprisingly liberating; it may even bring you a new measure of peace.

- Just get your body moving in whatever way you can, whenever you can, whether you're alone in an empty room or with a crowd of people at a wedding or taking ballroom dance classes. Don't worry, no one is watching you; and if they are, they're just jealous that they can't move the way you do, can't free themselves the way you can!

- And above all, dance as though your life depended on it, because it just might.

endnotes

[1]S. Glum. "Let It Be." *Damn Near Killed Him*. WordPress.com. November 24, 2007. Retrieved from http://damnednearkilledhim.wordpress.com/2007/11/24/let-it-be/.

[2]Jeremiah 9:20. Holy Bible. The Lockman Foundation, 1995.

[3]Dr. Gabor Maté, "Caring for ourselves when we care for others." March 6, 2013. Lecture. Retrieved from www.youtube.com/watch?v=c6IL8WVyMMs.

[4]Jeremiah 9:17. Holy Bible.

[5]Dr. Gabor Maté, *When the Body Says No* (Toronto: A.A. Knopf Canada, 2003) 244.

[6]www.cancer.org/treatment/childrenandcancer/helpingchildrenwhenafamilymemberhascancer/dealingwithaparentsterminalillness/dealing-with-a-parents-terminal-illness-surviving-parent-grief. Accessed July 13, 2014.

[7]Elisabeth Kübler-Ross, *On Death and Dying* (New York: Macmillan, 1969).

[8]Maurice Sendak, *Where the Wild Things Are* (New York: Harper Collins, 1991).

[9]Sandra Vander Schaaf, *Passionate Embrace: Faith, Flesh and Tango* (Toronto: Clements Publishing Group, Inc., 2013).

[10]Elisabeth Kübler-Ross, *Death: The Final Stage of Growth* (New York, NY: Wiley, John & Sons, Incorporated 1975).

[11]W.S. Gilbert and Arthur Sullivan. *The Mikado*. (1885).

[12]Madeleine L'Engle, *Walking on Water* (Wheaton, Illinois: Harold Shaw Publishers, 1980), 23.

[13]Dr. Gabor Maté, "Beyond the Medical Model." February 12, 2012. Lecture. Retrieved from www.youtube.com/watch?v=NRmSfXulwhI. Accessed October 27, 2013.

[14]Henry Havelock Ellis, *The Dance of Life* (Boston: Houghton Mifflin Company, 1923), Ch. 2.

[15]Agnes De Mille, *The Life and Work of Martha Graham: A Biography* (Random House, 1991), 264.

[16]Norman Cousins, *Anatomy of an Illness: As Perceived by the Patient* (New York: W.W. Norton, 1970), 47-48.

[17]Eleanor Cardozo, Go for Glory Conference, Harpenden, UK, July 2012. Lecture: "Beauty and the Arts."

[18]Aylmer Maude, *The Life of Tolstoy Later Years* (White Fish, MT: Kessinger Publishing, 2007), Appendix 1.

[19]As quoted in *Voices of Truth: Conversations with Scientists, Thinkers, and Healers* (2000) by Nina L. Diamond, 429; no publication of this statement has been located prior to its use in the film *Powder* (1995) written by Victor Salva, where it is presented as a quote of Einstein. Retrieved from http://en.wikiquote.org/wiki/Talk:Albert_Einstein. Accessed December 14, 2013.

[20]Anita Diamant, *The Red Tent* (New York: St. Martin's Press, 1997).

[21]Dr. Libby Weaver, Lecture: USANA conference, Richmond, BC, February 23, 2012. Lecture: "Stress, Happiness and Hormones."

[22]M.A. Price et al., "The Role of Psychosocial Factors in the Development of Breast Carcinoma. Part II: Life event stressors, social support, defense style, and emotional control and their interactions," *Cancer*, 91(4): 686-97.

[23]Ibid.

[24]M. Kosfeld, M. Heinrichs, P.J. Zak, U. Fischbacher, and E. Fehr, "Oxytocin increases trust in humans," *Nature*, 435(7042): 673–76. doi:10.1038/nature03701. PMID 15931222.

[25]Cousins, 89.

[26]Brene Brown, "The Power of Vulnerability." December 2010. Lecture (TED Talk). Retrieved from www.ted.com/talks/brene_brown_on_vulnerability.

[27]Paul Brand and Philip Yancey, (1993). *Pain: The Gift Nobody Wants* (Grand Rapids, Michigan: Zondervan, 1993), 12.

[28]Brown, "The Power of Vulnerability."

[29]Maté, *When the Body Says No*, 244.

[30]Eugene Didier, *Edgar Allan Poe Life and Poems: A New Memoir* (White Fish, MT: Kessinger Publishing, 2008) 101.

[31]CBC News, "A History of Residential Schools in Canada." CBCNews/ Canada [online] May 16, 2008. www.cbc.ca/news/canada/a-history-of-

residential-schools-in-canada-1.702280.

[32]Government of Canada. Ottawa: *Minister of Public Works and Government Services Canada. Aboriginal mental health and well-being. In The human face of mental health and mental illness in Canada* (Chapter 12, 2006). Retrieved from www.phac-aspc.gc.ca/publicat/human-humain06/index-eng.php.

[33]Bruce Cockburn, "Lovers in a Dangerous Time." Bruce Cockburn, *Stealing Fire*. True North Records, 1984.

[34]Sir John A. Macdonald Papers, volume 91, "Report on Industrial Schools for Indians and Half-Breeds" *The Davin Report* (14 March 1879) 35428-45.

[35]John and Paula Sandford, *The Transformation of the Inner Man* (Tulsa, OK Victory House Inc. 1962).

[36]Charles Dickens, *Great Expectations* (London: Chapman & Hall, 1861).

[37]Don Richardson, *Peace Child* (Glendale, California: Regal Books Division/G/L Publications, 1974) 206.

[38]Kenneth S. Saladin, *Anatomy and Physiology of the Autonomic Nervous System*, 6th edition (New York: McGraw-Hill, 2007).

[39]Leia N. Ambra, "Approaches Used in Dance/movement Therapy with Adult Women Incest Survivors," *American Journal of Dance Therapy*, 17(1): 15-24.

[40]S. Amir, Z.W. Brown, and Z. Amit, "The role of endorphins in stress: Evidence and speculations," *Newsletter & Biobehavioural Reviews*, 4 (November 2 1979): 77-86.

[41]C.B. Pert and S.H. Snyder, "Opiate receptor: demonstration in nervous tissue," *Science*, 179(4077) (March 1973): 1011-14.

[42]Candace Pert, *Molecules of Emotion: The Science Behind Mind-Body Medicine* (New York: Simon and Schuster, 1997).

[43]Dr. Dan Allender, *The Wounded Heart* (Colorado Springs, Colorado: Navpress, 1990), 154.

[44]Dr. Carol Burckhardt, Fibromyalgia Information Foundation. www.fibromyalgia.com.

[45]Fibromyalgia data: F. Wolfe, "Fibromyalgia: the clinical syndrome," *Rheumatic Disease Clinics of North America*, 15(1) (February 1989): 1-18. PMID 2644671. D.J. Wallace and D.S. Hallegua, "Fibromyalgia: The

gastrointestinal link." *Current Pain Headache Reports*, 8(5) (October 2002): 364-8. doi:10.1007/s11916-996-0009-z. PMID 15361320. D.J. Clauw, M. Schmidt, D. Radulovic, A. Singer, P. Katz, and J. Bresette, "The relationship between fibromyalgia and interstitial cystitis," *Journal of Psychiatric Research*, 31(1): 125-31. doi:10.101/S0022-3956(96)00051-9. PMID 9201654. R.W. Simms and D.L. Goldenberg, "Symptoms mimicking neurologic disorders in fibromyalgia syndrome," *Journal of Rheumatology*, 15(8): 1271-73. PMID 3184073.

[46]J. Hughes, H.W. Kosterlitz, T.W. Smith, "The distribution of methionine-enkephalin and leucine-enkephalin in the brain and peripheral tissues," *British Journal of Pharmacology*, 120(4): 428-436; discussion 436-37.

[47]Mary Battiata, "20/20: Inside Romanian Orphanages," *Washington Post*, October 5, 1990.

[48]Stephanie Pappas, "Early Neglect Alters Kids' Brains," LiveScience (July 23, 2012). Retrieved from www.livescience.com/21778-early-neglect-alters-kids-brains.html.

[49]Maté, *When the Body says No*, 6-9.

[50]Bruce Lipton, "The Biology of Belief." 2012. Lecture. Retrieved from www.youtube.com/watch?v=jjj0xVM4x1I.

[51]H. Lodish, D. Baltimore, A. Berk, S.L. Zipursky, P. Matsudaira, and J. Darnell. *Molecular Cell Biology* (Oxford: W H Freeman and Company, 1996).

[52]L. Stryer, *Biochemistry*, 4th edition (New York, NY: W.H. Freeman).

[53]G.M. Cooper and R. E. Hausman. *The Cell: A Molecular Approach*, 3rd edition (Washington, DC: ASM Press & Sunderland, MA: Sinauer Associates, 2004).

[54]U.R. Konigsberg, B.H. Lipton, and I.R. Konigsberg, "The regenerative response of single mature muscle fibers isolated in vitro," *Developmental Biology*, 45(2): 260-75.

[55]H. Mertz, V. Morgan, G. Tanner, et al., "Regional cerebral activation in irritable bowel syndrome and control subjects with painful and non-painful rectal distention," *Gastroenterology*, 18: 842-848.

[56]P. Luu and M. Posner, "Anterior cingulate cortex regulation of sympathetic activity," *Neuroscience from Oxford*, 126(10) 2119-2120.

[57]Dr. Gabor Maté, "Beyond the Medical Model."

[58]Robert M. Sapolsky, "Hippocampal Damage Associated with Prolonged Glucocorticoid Exposure in Primates," *The Journal of Neuroscience*, 10(9): 2897-2902.

[59]R.M. Thomas, G. Hotsenpiller, and D. Peterson, "Acute Psychosocial Stress Reduces Cell Survival in Adult Hippocampal Neurogenisis without altering Proliferation," *The Journal of Neuroscience*, 27(11): 2734-2743.

[60]H. Prigerson, A. Bierhals, S. Kasl, C. Reynolds, K. Shear, N. Day, L. Beery, J. Newsom, and S. Jacobs, "Traumatic Grief as a Risk Factor for Mental and Physical Morbidity," *American Journal of Psychiatry*, 154: 616-623.

[61]Joe Verghese, M.D., Richard B. Lipton, M.D., and Mindy J. Katz, M.P.H., "Leisure Activities and the Risk of Dementia in the Elderly," *New England Journal of Medicine*, 348: 2508-2516.

[62]A.K. LePort, A.T. Mattfeld, H. Dickinson-Anson, J.H. Fallon, C.E. Stark, F. Kruggel, L. Cahill, J.L. McGaugh. "Behavioral and neuroanatomical investigation of Highly Superior Autobiographical Memory (HSAM)," *Neurobiology of Learning and Memory*, 98(1): 78. DOI: 10.1016/j.nlm.2012.05.002.

[63]Mark Johnson, *The Body in the Mind: The Bodily Basis of Meaning, Imagination and Reason* (Chicago: University of Chicago Press, 1987).

[64]Cousins, 47-48.

[65]Cousins.

[66]J. Hughes, H.W. Kosterlitz, and T.W. Smith, "The distribution of methionine-enkephalin and leucine-enkephalin in the brain and peripheral tissues," *British Journal of Pharmacology*, 120(4): 428-436; discussion 436-437.

[67]Mitch Albom, *Tuesdays with Morrie* (New York: Doubleday, a division of Random House, 1997), 52.

[68]Tessa Hart, PhD, and Keith Cicerone, PhD, "Emotional Problems after Traumatic Brain Injury," brainline.org. 2010. Retrieved from www.brainline.org/content/2010/03/emotional-problems-after-traumatic-brain-injury_pageall.html.

[69]Tremblay v. Daigle 2 S.C.R. 530: Injunction against abortion: "A consideration of the status of the foetus under the Civil Code supports

the conclusion that a foetus is not a 'human being' under the Quebec Charter. The provisions of the Code providing for the appointment of a curator for an unborn child and the provisions granting patrimonial interests to such child do not implicitly recognize that a foetus is a juridical person." 1989.

[70]Barbara Kingsolver, *Poisonwood Bible* (New York: Harper Collins Publishers, 1998), 830.

[71]Brene Brown. Interview. Retrieved from www.theworkofthepeople.com/jesus-wept.

[72]Barbara Ehrenreich, *Dancing in the Streets: A History of Collective Joy* (New York, NY: Metropolitan Books, Henry Holt and Company, 2006). 77.

[73]Glynis Sherwood, "Chronic 'Stuck' Grief: 10 warning& 5 vital healing strategies." Blog: Glynis Sherwood Counseling. October 15, 2012. www.glynissherwood.com/blog/chronic-'stuck'-grief-10-warning-signs-5-vital-healing-strategies.

[74]Brand and Yancey.

[75]Luke 2:9. Holy Bible. King James Version (London: Church of England, 1611/www.thebible.co.uk).

[76]"Trauma" *Apple Dictionary*

[77]S. Glum, S. "Bag of Gold." *Damn Near Killed Him*. WordPress.com. April 15, 2008. Retrieved from http://damnednearkilledhim.wordpress.com/2008/04/15/a-bag-of-gold.

[78]Canadian Race Relations Foundation: "From Racism to Redress: The Japanese Canadian Experience." www.crr.ca/divers-files/en/pub/faSh/ePubFaShRacRedJap.pdf.

[79]Fyodor Dostoyevsky, *Crime and Punishment*. Trans. Sidney Monas (New York: Signet Classics/Penguin, 1968).

[80]Jeremiah 31:12-13. Holy Bible.

[81]Anne Lamott, *Plan B: Further Thoughts on Faith* (New York: Riverhead Books. 2005), 174.

[82]C.S. Lewis, *A Grief Observed* (London: Faber and Faber, 1961). 7.

[83]Lamott, 174.

references and further reading

Albom, Mitch. 1997. *Tuesdays with Morrie* (New York: Doubleday, a division of Random House).

Allender, Dan. 1990. *The Wounded Heart* (Colorado Springs, Colorado: Navpress).

Ambra, Leia N. Spring/Summer 1995. "Approaches Used in Dance/movement Therapy with Adult Women Incest Survivors." *American Journal of Dance Therapy*, 17(1): 15-24.

Amir S., Brown Z.W., and Amit Z., November 2, 1979. "The role of endorphins in stress: Evidence and Speculations." *Newsletter & Biobehavioural Reviews*, 4: 77-86.

LePort, A.K., Mattfeld, A.T., Dickinson-Anson, H., Fallon, J.H., Stark, C.E., Kruggel, F., Cahill, L., and McGaugh, J.L. 2012. "Behavioral and Neuroanatomical Investigation of Highly Superior Autobiographical Memory (HSAM)." *Neurobiology of Learning and Memory*, 98(1): 78.

Battiata, Mary. October 5, 1990. "20/20: Inside Romanian Orphanages." *Washington Post*.

Brand, Paul, and Yancey, Philip. (1993). *Pain: The Gift Nobody Wants* (Grand Rapids, Michigan: Zondervan).

Burckhardt, Carol. Fibromyalgia Information Foundation. www.fibromyalgia.com

CBC News Transcript. May 16, 2008. "A History of Residential Schools in Canada." CBCNews/Canada [online]. www.cbc.ca/news/canada/a-history-of-residential-schools-in-canada-1.702280

Canadian Race Relations Foundation. [n.d.]. "From Racism to Redress: The Japanese Canadian Experience." www.crr.ca/divers-files/en/pub/faSh/ePubFaShRacRedJap.pdf

Clauw, D.J., Schmidt, M., Radulovic, D., Singer, A., Katz, P., and Bresette, J. (January–February 1997). "The relationship between fibromyalgia and interstitial cystitis." *Journal of Psychiatric Research*, 3(1).

Cooper, G.M., and Hausman, R.E. 2004. *The Cell: A Molecular Approach*, 3rd edition (Washington, DC: ASM Press & Sunderland, MA: Sinauer Associates).

Cousins, Norman. 1970. *Anatomy of an Illness: As Perceived by the Patient* (New York: W.W. Norton).

Davin Report. March 14, 1879. "Report on Industrial Schools for Indians and Half-Breeds."

De Mille, Agnes. 1991. *The Life and Work of Martha Graham: A Biography* (New York: Random House).

Diamant, Anita. 1997. *The Red Tent* (New York: St. Martin's Press).

Dickens, Charles. 1861/2008. *Great Expectations* (London: Chapman & Hall).

Didier, Eugene. 1879/2008 *Edgar Allan Poe Life and Poems : A New Memoir* (White Fish, MT: Kessinger Publishing).

Dostoyevsky, Fyodor. 1968. *Crime and Punishment*.Trans. Sidney Monas (New York: Signet Classics/Penguin).

Ehrenreich, Barbara. 2006. *Dancing in the Streets: A History of Collective Joy* (New York, NY: Metropolitan Books, Henry Holt and Company).

Glum, Sandy. 2007. "Let It Be." *Damn Near Killed Him.* WordPress.com. http://damnednearkilledhim.wordpress.com/2007/11/24/let-it-be

Government of Canada. Ottawa: Minister of Public Works and Government Services Canada. Aboriginal mental health and well-being. In The human face of mental health and mental illness in Canada (Chapter 12, 2006). www.phac-aspc.gc.ca/publicat/human-humain06/index-eng.php

Hart, Tessa, PhD, and Cicerone, Keith, PhD. "Emotional Problems After Traumatic Brain Injury." brainline.org. www.brainline.org/content/2010/03/emotional-problems-after-traumatic-brain-injury_pageall.html

Havelock Ellis, Henry. 1923/1973.*The Dance of Life* (Westport, CT: Greenwood Press).

Hughes, J., Kosterlitz, H.W., and Smith, T.W.1997. "The distribution of methionine-enkephalin and leucine-enkephalin in the brain and peripheral tissues." *British Journal of Pharmacology,* 120(4): 428–436.

Johnson, Mark. 1987.*The Body in the Mind: The Bodily Basis of Meaning, Imagination and Reason* (Chicago: The University of Chicago Press).

Kingsolver, Barbara. 1998. *Poisonwood Bible* (New York: Harper Collins

Publishers).

Konigsberg U.R., Lipton B.H., and Konigsberg I.R. August 1975. "The Regenerative Response of single mature muscle fibers isolated in vitro." *Developmental Biology*, 45(2): 260-75.

Kosfeld M., Heinrichs M., Zak P.J. ,Fischbacher U., and Fehr E. June 2005. "Oxytocin increases trust in humans." *Nature*, 435(7042): 673-76. doi:10.1038/nature03701. PMID 15931222.

Kübler-Ross, Elisabeth. 1969. *On Death and Dying* (New York: Macmillan).

Lamott, Anne. 2005. *Plan B: Further Thoughts on Faith* (New York: Riverhead Books).

L'Engle, Madeleine. 1980. *Walking on Water* (Wheaton, Illinois: Harold Shaw Publishers).

Lewis, C.S. 1961. *A Grief Observed* (London: Faber and Faber).

Lodish H., Baltimore D., Berk A., Zipursky S.L., Matsudaira P., and Darnell J. 1996. *Molecular Cell Biology* (Oxford: W H Freeman and Company).

Luu, P., and Posner, M. October 2003. "Anterior cingulate cortex regulation of sympathetic activity." *Neuroscience from Oxford*, 126(10): 2119-2120.

Maté, Gabor M.D. 2003. *When the Body Says No* (Toronto: A.A. Knopf Canada).

Maude, Aylmer. 2007. *The Life of Tolstoy Later Years* (White Fish, MT: Kessinger Publishing.

Mertz H., Morgan V., Tanner G., et al. 2000. "Regional cerebral activation in irritable bowel syndrome and control subjects with painful and non-painful rectal distention." *Gastroenterology*, 1(18):842-848.

Pappas, Stephanie. July 23, 2012. "Early Neglect Alters Kids' Brains." *LiveScience*. www.livescience.com/21778-early-neglect-alters-kids-brains. html

Pert, Candace. 1997. *Molecules of Emotion: The Science Behind Mind-Body Medicine* (New York: Simon and Schuster).

Pert, C.B., Snyder, S.H. March 1973. "Opiate receptor: demonstration in nervous tissue." *Science*, 179(4077): 1011-14.

Prigerson, H., Bierhals, A., Kasl, S., Reynolds, C., Shear, K., Day, N.,

Beery, L., Newsom J., and Jacobs S. 1997. "Traumatic Grief as a Risk Factor for Mental and Physical Morbidity." *American Journal of Psychiatry*, 154:616-623.

Price M.A., et al. February 15, 2001. "The Role of Psychosocial Factors in the Development of Breast Carcinoma. Part II: Life event stressors, social support, defense style, and emotional control and their interactions." *Cancer*, 4(15): 686-97.

Richardson, Don. 1974. *Peace Child* (Glendale, California: Regal Books Division/G/L Publications).

Sandford, John and Paula. 1962. *The Transformation of the Inner Man* (Tulsa, OK Victory House Inc.).

Sapolsky, Robert M. September 1990. "Hippocampal Damage Associated with Prolonged Glucocorticoid Exposure in Primates." *The Journal of Neuroscience*, 10(9): 2897-2902.

Sendak, Maurice. 1991. *Where the Wild Things Are* (New York: Harper Collins).

Simms, R.W., and Goldenberg, D.L. August 1988. "Symptoms mimicking neurologic disorders in fibromyalgia syndrome." *Journal of Rheumatology*, 15(8): 1271-73. PMID 3184073.

Sherwood, Glynis. "Chronic 'Stuck' Grief: 10 warning & 5 vital healing strategies." Blog: Glynis Sherwood Counseling. www.glynissherwood. com/blog/chronic-d.com/blog/chronic-%2525E2%252580%252598stuc k%2525E2%2525

Stryer, L. 1995. *Biochemistry*, 4th edition (New York, NY: W.H. Freeman).

Thomas R.M., Hotsenpiller, G., and Peterson, D. March 14, 2007. "Acute Psychosocial Stress Reduces Cell Survival in Adult Hippocampal Neurogenisis without altering Proliferation." *The Journal of Neuroscience*, 27(11): 2734-2743.

Vander Schaaf, Sandra. 2013. *Passionate Embrace: Faith, Flesh and Tango* (Toronto: Clements Publishing Group, Inc.).

Verghese, Joe, M.D., Lipton, Richard B., M.D., and Katz, Mindy J., M.P.H. June 19, 2003. "Leisure Activities and the Risk of Dementia in the Elderly." *New England Journal of Medicine*, 348:2508-2516.

Wallace D.J., and Hallegua, D.S. October 2002. "Fibromyalgia: the gastrointestinal link." *Current Pain Headache Reports*, 8(5): 364–68.

doi:10.1007/s11916-996-0009-z. PMID 15361320.

Kenneth S. Saladin, *Anatomy and Physiology of the Autonomic Nervous System*, 6th edition (New York: McGraw-Hill, 2007).

Wolfe, F. February 1989. "Fibromyalgia: the clinical syndrome." *Rheumatic Disease Clinics of North America*, 15(1): 1–18. PMID 2644671.

Video

Brown, Brene. "The Power of Vulnerability." TED Talk. December 2010. Lecture. Accessed October 14, 2013. Retrieved from www.ted.com/talks/brene_brown_on_vulnerability

Brown, Brene. Interview. Accessed February 27, 2014. Retrieved from www.theworkofthepeople.com/jesus-wept

Lipton, Bruce. "The Biology of Belief." 2012. Lecture. Accessed November 18, 2013. Retrieved from www.youtube.com/watch?v=jjj0xVM4x1I

Maté, Gabor, M.D. "Caring for ourselves when we care for others." March 6, 2013. Lecture. Accessed October 24, 2013. Retrieved from www.youtube.com/watch?v=c6IL8WVyMMs

Maté, Gabor, M.D. "Beyond the Medical Model". February 12, 2012. Lecture. Accessed October 27, 2013. Retrieved from www.youtube.com/watch?v=NRmSfXulwhI

Made in the USA
Charleston, SC
14 September 2014